OPPORTUNITIES

in

Museum
Careers

OPPORTUNITIES

in

Museum
Careers

REVISED EDITION

BLYTHE CAMENSON

New York   Chicago   San Francisco   Lisbon   London   Madrid   Mexico City
Milan   New Delhi   San Juan   Seoul   Singapore   Sydney   Toronto

Library of Congress Cataloging-in-Publication Data

Camenson, Blythe.
    Opportunities in museums careers / by Blythe Camenson. — Rev. ed.
        p.   cm.
    Includes bibliographical references (p.).
    ISBN 0-07-146769-6 (alk. paper)
        1. Museums—Vocational guidance—United States.   I. Title: Museum careers.
    II. Title.

    AM11.C35   2007
    069'.023—dc22   2005037409

1 2 3 4 5 6 7 8 9 10 11 12 13 14 15 16 17 18 19 20   DOC/DOC   0 9 8 7 6

ISBN-13: 978-0-07-146769-8
ISBN-10:   0-07-146769-6

Interior design by Rattray Design

McGraw-Hill books are available at special quantity discounts to use as premiums and sales promotions, or for use in corporate training programs. For more information, please write to the Director of Special Sales, Professional Publishing, McGraw-Hill, Two Penn Plaza, New York, NY 10121-2298. Or contact your local bookstore.

This book is printed on acid-free paper.

To Anna Beach, my favorite museum lover

Contents

FOREWORD

ON SATURDAYS, WHEN I was a child, my parents used to drive my brother and me downtown to the Newark Museum for art classes. They thought that it was important to expose us to art and history. For my brother and me it was just fun. We weren't particularly interested in culture. I'm sure we didn't even know what it was. We loved to walk through the huge galleries filled with paintings, sculpture, and pottery. Like every child, our favorite exhibit was always the mummy—a real person who was swaddled in bandages and had painted toes and a beautiful golden mask. "Do you suppose she was a queen?" my brother would ask. "Do you suppose she rode down the Nile?" Our imaginations took flight.

In the art rooms, we wore old shirts and created pictures like those we had seen in the corridors of the museum. Sometimes we added feathers or glitter or buttons stuck down with white glue. Sometimes we created papier-mâché sculptures that took several weeks to dry before they could be brought home. My brother would draw pictures of Cleopatra riding majestically down the Nile River as he supposed the mummy in the case had once done. I remember those Saturdays of wonder and amazement, and I suppose that in some subconscious way they helped me to choose museum work as my profession. My brother became an artist.

Now that I am older, I know that museums are about more than just "neat stuff," although it was the opportunity to touch the past and to imagine a different place and time that originally fascinated me. In our society, museums serve the function of putting us in touch with other cultures, with faraway places and people. They preserve the things of time past, the products of human existence—creativity, beauty, cruelty and defeat, celebration and triumph, everyday life. They tell us about who we are and how we came to be as we are. Like the shamans among indigenous people in the rain forests of South America, who collect and pass on the traditions of centuries of their people's existence, museums are storehouses of knowledge and culture. They protect and preserve our collective identity and memory. But today museums can be something even more. Unlike more formal institutions of learning, museums are like universities for the entire community. They can open our eyes to ideas. They can use objects as catalysts for discussion and debate. Museum exhibitions can encourage us to understand one another, bringing people of different backgrounds together to reason and solve problems. Museums can be community resources and centers for action within the community.

These examples illustrate the role of the museum as community forum, educator, and bridge builder. The Weeksville Society in the middle of Bedford Stuyvesant, Brooklyn, New York, developed a preservation program that trained people in the neighborhood to become restoration carpenters. Once trained, the restoration carpenters trained others. This model project benefited the museum and helped to address the problem of training unskilled workers, one job at a time. In the same city, the Brooklyn Children's Museum provides after-school education programs for children who might otherwise be on the streets or home alone while their parents are at work. This involvement in the community helps parents, protects the community's children, and provides them with experiential education in art and science. In conjunction with an exhibition about the periodically explosive relationship between African-Americans and American Jews, the Jewish Museum in New York City developed an education program that brought children from a variety of backgrounds together to create art. The project resulted in a decision by the students to learn more about one another and to visit one another's schools. One visitor to the exhibition wrote, "As an American Jew, I feel a new connection to African-Americans . . . After viewing this exhibition, I have a different perspective." Another wrote, "You have built a bridge that breaks down boundaries."

Those of us who work in museums today and those of us who train museum professionals, as I do, see museums as exciting and dynamic places to work. As we look ahead to the future of museums, we see more than simply storehouses of art and history: we see places that can break down boundaries and build bridges among people. If ideas and artifacts excite you, then this book is the first step in your journey toward a career in museums.

Gretchen Sullivan Sorin
Director
Cooperstown Graduate Program in History Museum Studies

ACKNOWLEDGMENTS

The AUTHOR WOULD like to thank the following museum professionals for providing information for this book:

Don Albro, Director, Joseph Smith Historic Center
Patricia Baker, Wardrobe and Textiles Manager, Plimoth
    Plantation
Tom Bernardin, Interpretive Ranger, Ellis Island
Kent Brinkley, Landscape Architect, Colonial
    Williamsburg
Matthew Carone, Artist/Owner, Carone Gallery
Aileen Chuk, Associate Registrar, Metropolitan Museum
    of Art
Mary Alice Dwyer, Volunteer Coordinator, Museum of
    Science, Boston
John Fleckner, Chief Archivist, Smithsonian Institution
Jeremy Fried, Character Interpreter, Colonial
    Williamsburg

Joan Gardner, Chief Conservator, Carnegie Museum of
Natural History

Tom Gerhardt, Cooper/Character Interpreter, Plimoth
Plantation

Hank Grasso, Exhibit Designer, National Museum of
American History, Smithsonian Institution

Wesley Greene, Landscape Supervisor, Colonial
Williamsburg

Noreen Grice, Operations Coordinator/Astronomer,
Charles Hayden Planetarium, Museum of Science,
Boston

Erica Hirshler, Assistant Curator, Museum of Fine Arts,
Boston

James King, Director, Carnegie Museum of Natural
History

Kendra Lambert, Former Student Intern, National
Museum of American History, Smithsonian Institution

Deb Mason, Potter, Plimoth Plantation

Charles McGovern, Curator, National Museum of
American History, Smithsonian Institution

Judy Negip, Public Relations Coordinator, Museum of Fine
Arts, Boston

Joel Pontz, Artisan/Character Interpreter, Plimoth
Plantation

Mike Sarna, Collections Manager, Museum of Science and
Industry, Chicago

Larry Schindler, Director, Charles Hayden Planetarium,
Museum of Science, Boston

Jeremy Slavitz, Docent, Nantucket Historical Association

Carolyn Travers, Director of Research, Plimoth Plantation

Joyce Williams, Director of Special Projects, Museum of
Discovery and Science, Fort Lauderdale, Florida
Gordie Wilson, Superintendent, Castillo de San Marcos
National Monument, St. Augustine, Florida

The editors would like to gratefully acknowledge the contribution of Josephine Scanlon, a freelance writer and editor specializing in career topics, for preparing this revised edition.

1

THE WORLD OF MUSEUMS

IF YOU ASK some people what they think of museums, they might
tell you that the word conjures up images of yawn-stifling tours in
quiet, tomblike places, the atmosphere as inspiring as the inside of
a crypt. The idea of displaying and examining the art and artifacts
that make up the world's history reminds them of dry school les-
sons filled with impossible-to-remember names and dates and
events that hold no meaning in their current lives.

Fortunately, that perception is not as widely shared as those
uninitiated in the wonders of museums might believe. But if you
are reading this book, you already know that. Museums are not dull
and lifeless structures displaying dull and lifeless artifacts. They are
as exciting as a space launch or a Civil War battlefield, an African
safari or a Roman amphitheater.

Patrons of the arts, history lovers, and those who look to the
future have continuously provided enthusiastic support to museums, ensuring their survival through the ages. From meager begin-

nings, thousands of museums now flourish throughout the world, and they display a wide range of collections.

Museums are no longer repositories for just art or ancient relics. They house everything from moon rocks to Julia Childs's kitchen. And as varied as the collections are, so are the opportunities for employment. In the pages ahead we will explore the different kinds of museums, their goals and focuses, and the career paths they offer. But first a brief history lesson.

How Museums Originated

The word *museum* comes from the ancient Greek name for the temple of the Muses, who were the nine patron goddesses of the arts in Greek mythology. The term was first used to refer to institutions of advanced learning, and it did not take on its current meaning until the Renaissance, when the first great collections of art were formed in Italy. During the seventeenth and eighteenth centuries, art museums thrived in Europe. As in the Renaissance period, however, almost all collections were private and offered limited public access.

One private museum was the collection of Sir Hans Sloane, which was bequeathed to Great Britain in 1753. It became the foundation for the British Museum, the first museum organized as a public institution.

In the late 1800s, several specialized museums were created in European cities, including the Bavarian National Museum in Munich and the Museum of Ornamental Art in London, which was later renamed the Victoria and Albert Museum. The first museums to be established as public institutions in the United States were the Museum of Fine Arts in Boston in 1870, the Metropolitan Museum of Art in New York City in 1872, and the Art Institute of Chicago in 1879.

Different Kinds of Museums

Today there are as many different kinds of museums as the topics they explain or the items they display. Some are famous establishments, such as the museums of the Smithsonian Institution; others are small establishments, known only locally. This chapter will give you an overview of each type of museum; the roles they play and the job opportunities they provide will be examined in greater detail in the chapters to follow.

Art Museums

Art museums are buildings where objects of aesthetic value are preserved and displayed. Art museums have many functions including acquiring, conserving, and exhibiting works of art; providing art education for the general public; and conducting art historical research.

Since the beginning of the twentieth century, art museums have seen a number of trends, including the expansion of large institutions and the creation of specialized museums, many of which are devoted to modern art. In contrast, a number of the world's largest museums have begun to reduce their size and improve the quality of their collections. They accomplish this by selling less-important works of art and concentrating available funds on acquiring works of greater artistic merit or historical significance.

Art Galleries

Art galleries are generally privately owned and are similar to specialized museums in which the collection is restricted to the works of a single artist. Art galleries can also focus on a specific historical period, category of art, or geographical region.

History Museums

From acquiring collections and preserving them to explaining and displaying them, the dedicated professionals employed in history museums have the chance to work with every aspect of the relics and other forms of physical evidence of the past. History museums can cover a particular period, such as colonial America, or a particular topic, such as entertainment or advertising. A history museum's collection could be displayed in a modern building constructed specifically for that purpose; or the building itself, along with its contents, could be historical. Examples include the homes of famous people such as Paul Revere or Thomas Jefferson or historic structures such as lighthouses or old courthouses.

Living History Museums

A living history museum is a vibrant, active village, town, or city where the day-to-day life of a particular time period has been authentically re-created. The houses and public buildings are restored originals or thoroughly researched reproductions. Interiors are outfitted with period furniture, cookware, bed linens, and tablecloths.

Employees known as *character interpreters* function as residents, wearing the clothing of their day and discussing their dreams and concerns with visitors as they go about their daily tasks. If you were to stop a costumed gentleman passing by and ask where the nearest McDonald's is, he would not have any idea what you were talking about—unless he thought to direct you to a neighbor's farm. He might even do so using the dialect of his home country.

Colonial Williamsburg in Virginia and Plimoth Plantation in Massachusetts are just two examples of living history museums.

These large enterprises offer employment for professional and entry-level workers in a wide variety of categories.

Natural History Museums

Natural history museums are dedicated to research, exhibition, and education in the natural sciences. Such museums vary in size and collections and could include all or some of the following departments: anthropology, astronomy, botany, entomology, fossil and living vertebrates, geology, herpetology and ichthyology, mammalogy, mineralogy, ornithology, and vertebrate paleontology.

Collections may include artifacts from ancient civilizations, gems and jewels, fossils, meteorites, and animals from around the world displayed in lifelike settings.

Science Museums and Discovery Centers

Science museums preserve and display objects that have been important to the development of science and technology. Science centers, or discovery centers as they are also sometimes called, generally teach the principles related to these fields. They often involve visitors in hands-on activities, and many such museums and centers cater particularly to children. The two types of science museums are not mutually exclusive, although most institutions fall into one category or the other.

Planetariums

Planetariums are structures, usually with domed ceilings, that are outfitted to give audiences the illusion of being outside under a starlit sky. Through the use of projectors, slides, movies, and computers, the locations of the planets and stars and all other sorts of astronomical activity can be demonstrated.

Planetariums are often part of a science museum complex, with most large cities now having full-scale facilities. They are used as tourist and educational attractions and have elaborate space exhibits or public observational facilities. Smaller planetariums are also associated with universities and are used for classroom instruction in geography, navigation, and astronomy.

National Historic Sites

National historic sites and monuments, such as the Statue of Liberty and Ellis Island, are operated by the National Park Service, which falls under the umbrella of the U.S. Department of the Interior. These federally funded museums offer a wide range of full-time and seasonal employment for interpretive rangers and other personnel.

Canada also has an extensive national park system with nearly one thousand sites throughout the country.

Archives and Genealogy

Archives handle collections that chart the course of daily life for individuals and businesses. Some archives specifically look after the materials created by their own institution. For example, years ago the Coca-Cola Company established an archive to have a history of what the company business was and how it had prospered over the years. New companies set up archives to keep a documented record of their progress. Other institutions, such as universities or museums, create archives that relate to what their special research interests are.

Genealogy is the field of study that delves into the past to trace family roots. Genealogical research is important to researchers in living history museums and is also of value to the work of archivists.

Other Museums

Museums deal with tangible objects, both inanimate and animate. Other categories exist in addition to the types of museums listed above. The American Association of Museums (AAM) includes arboreta and botanic gardens and zoos and aquariums in its definition of a museum.

Other museums cover only a specific item, event, or phenomenon or cater to a particular audience. The Rock 'n' Roll Museum in Cleveland, the Holocaust Museum in Washington, DC, the Teddy Bear Museum in Fort Myers, Florida, the D-Day Museum in New Orleans, and museums developed specifically for children are examples of these.

Jobs in Museums

Professional job classifications within museums can fall into several categories including administration, collections, curation, education and interpretation, development (fund-raising), exhibit design, and research.

In addition, museums employ a large team of support staff including security guards, maintenance workers, groundskeepers, landscape architects, and secretarial and other office workers.

Many job titles are common to each kind of museum, but the job description will vary depending on the institution. Curators, exhibit designers, and registrars, for example, are found in almost every type of museum, from art to science to history museums, even though the collections they deal with and their specific duties are very different. Taxidermists, on the other hand, are usually found only in natural history or science museums, where their specialized skills are most needed.

The AAM has identified dozens of both direct and museum-related career categories. Here is a list of the jobs examined in this book. For easy reference, the chapter numbers in which the jobs are discussed are enclosed in parentheses after the title.

Job Title
Archaeologist (6)
Architectural conservator (5)
Architectural historian (5)
Archivist (10)
Art gallery owner (3)
Artisan (5, 6)
CAD systems professional (6)
Character interpreter (5)
Collections manager (3, 6, 7)
Conservator (3, 6, 7)
Costumer (5)
Curator (3, 4, 7)
Director (4, 6, 7)
Editor/writer (6)
Educator (6)
Exhibit builder (6)
Exhibit designer (4, 6)
Genealogist (10)
Groundskeeper (5)
Historic interiors designer (5)

Landscape preservationist (5)
Librarian (3)
Marketing director (3)
Park ranger (9)
Photographer (3, 6)
Preparator (4)
Presenter (5)
Public relations coordinator (3)
Registrar (3, 7)
Researcher (5)
Scientific illustrator (6)
Taxidermist (6)
Tour guide/docent (3, 4, 6)
Volunteer coordinator (6)

Choosing a Museum Career

With so many different kinds of museums and the varied job categories they support, how do you know which avenue would be right for you? Take a look at the chart that follows below. Find your interests and skills, and then look across to identify career options. You will see that many of the job titles combine more than one interest.

Interests and Skills	*Job Titles*
Working with your hands	Archaeologist, archivist, artisan, costumer, curator of structures, exhibit builder, exhibit designer, landscape archaeologist, restoration architect, taxidermist

Finding out information	Archaeologist, archivist, astronomer, curator, genealogist, historian, landscape archaeologist, researcher, scientist
Working with the public	Art gallery owner, character interpreter, educator, information officer, marketing director, park ranger, public relations coordinator, security guide, tour guide
Working outdoors	Archaeologist, character interpreter, curator of structures, park ranger, restoration architect, tour guide
Working with historic buildings	Architectural historian, curator, curator of structures, exhibit designer, historic interiors specialist, preservationist, restoration architect

Qualifications You Will Need

The required qualifications for museum work vary depending on the job. Although many employers prefer their applicants to have a bachelor's or higher degree in any number of fields, not all do. Often the following qualifications are considered much more important: experience, extensive knowledge of a particular time period or region, the ability to communicate with diverse groups of people, a pleasant demeanor, good writing skills, and research skills.

The Job Hunt

Although many museum lovers can find employment in their hometown—in a local historic house, museum, or art gallery, for example—to broaden your opportunities, chances are you will have to relocate. If you have a place in mind where you would like to work, a phone call or an introductory letter sent with your résumé is a good way to start.

Because many sites are state or federally operated, you might have to obtain a special application through the state capital or from Washington, DC. Some private employers, however, such as the Colonial Williamsburg Foundation, expect job hopefuls to apply directly. Information about job openings is listed on the organizations' websites.

Many professional associations produce monthly or quarterly newsletters with job listings and upcoming internships and fellowships. The websites of many such organizations also list job postings. Contact information for some key organizations is provided in Appendix A.

If you would like some more ideas on possible locations, the *Official Museum Directory*, put out by the AAM, is a valuable resource found in the reference section of most libraries. In addition to its many pages of history museums and historic houses, buildings, and sites, it lists scores of historical and preservation societies, boards, agencies, councils, commissions, foundations, and research industries. Using the information found in this resource, you could select a region where you would like to work and then gather the appropriate contact information for the appropriate organizations in that area.

The AAM also puts out a monthly newsletter called *Aviso*. Part of each issue is devoted to listings for employment opportunities and internships. Also, the AAM sponsors Aviso Museum Careers, an online resource that allows job seekers to post résumés and conduct job searches. The Web address is www.aam-us.org/aviso. Here are just a few examples of the types of jobs advertised in one issue. (Because these jobs are no longer open, the employers have not been identified.)

Museum Archivist—A public museum in Wisconsin is seeking a half-time archivist to manage its collection of materials related to local history. Minimum requirement of bachelor's degree in archives administration, U.S. history, or library science and three years professional experience.

Assistant to the Artistic Director—Assistant to the artistic director/founder of a world-renowned art museum and the director of an internationally known summer artist residency is sought. Top-notch administrative and business skills are essential, as are diverse and tireless social skills and a passion for twentieth-century art and artists. M.A. in art history preferred; business and arts administration courses a plus. Work involves assisting in arts administration, writing, editing, public relations, exhibition coordination, and supervision of contemporary art and archival video collection. Very good computer skills are a must. Candidates should have two to four years of work experience at prominent art museums, auction houses, and/or internationally known galleries.

Mobile Learning Center Outreach Specialist—Develop and lead tours for all age groups through temporary exhibitions installed on the Mobile Learning Center (MLC) (subjects include art, history, archaeology, and NASA-related programs); develop and maintain positive relationships with school administrators and teachers; promote the MLC to teachers and schedule visits when appropriate; develop educational materials for teachers; assist with research and installation of exhibitions on the MLC; drive the MLC and ensure routine maintenance is performed; work with and report to the curator of education.

Required qualifications include a bachelor's degree; experience working with children; excellent communication and organizational skills; a valid driver's license as well as excellent driving record; interest in art, history, archaeology, and science; ability to travel, including overnights; experience and understanding of customer service; and commitment to working with multicultural populations.

Preferred qualifications include experience in a museum or school setting; experience developing and/or delivering curriculum-based programs; and public speaking experience.

Art Writer/Editor—Director of a summer arts program seeks a writer/editor to help prepare a publication about this summer's arts residency. Strong writing and administrative skills are essential to the writer/editor position. This is project-based work with the possibility of full-time employment. The writer/editor will help compile and edit text on the program for comprehensive publication. Requirements include a minimum B.A. in art history or related field, M.A. preferred; willingness to travel; high-level editorial and publishing experience with regard to interviewing artists and integrating visual, textual, and archival material. A passion for contemporary art is a must.

Director—Director for historic house museum and garden. Seeking creative, energetic individual to oversee exciting house museum. Responsibilities include collections management, and exhibit and educational program development. Background in decorative arts and ability to work with board and volunteers is important.

Historian II—The state historical society of a northwest state is seeking a historian to manage the society's scholarly history magazine. Responsibilities include editing agency newsletters, developing materials for state historic sites, and providing assistance with planning the society's public programs. Minimum qualifications: M.A. in history, English, or journalism; proven experience in editing, design, and layout.

Salaries

Salaries vary widely from position to position, but they are generally low, as are most pay scales for education-related fields. Factors such as the source of funding or the geographic location of the museum determine salary levels more than does the complexity of the job or the level of a candidate's education and experience.

Some jobs pay only hourly wages; others follow the federal government's GS scale. A tour guide might earn $6.00 to $10.00 an hour, an assistant curator in the mid- to high twenties a year, and a restoration architect in the thirties to forties.

Most jobs provide benefits such as health insurance. But all those interviewed for this book stressed that financial rewards were not the main reason—or even a consideration—in pursuing their chosen professions. The low pay is far outweighed by the satisfaction of doing work they love.

Employment Outlook

Each year more and more historic buildings are nominated for inclusion on the National Register. Many of these sites are operated as historic house museums open to the public. This means that more and more employment opportunities are opening up for museum workers.

But history museums are not the only depositories expanding across the country. Art galleries and art museums can be found in almost any town; science museums, discovery centers, and planetariums are maintained in most mid- to large-size cities or university towns.

New job titles have been added to the list once limited to curators and librarians. The field of museum work is now open to all sorts of professionals, including restoration specialists, designers, planners, financiers, audience advocates, information specialists, and many more.

Although the competition in some sectors is stiff and funding always seems to lag behind public demand, a persistent museum lover can get his or her foot in the door through volunteering or participating in a student internship. The majority of professionals interviewed in this book report that the first step to landing their job was, indeed, a stint of volunteering or interning.

2

PREPARING FOR A
MUSEUM CAREER

WITH MUSEUMS OFFERING so many diverse careers, it stands to reason that avenues of training leading to these professions are equally diverse. An art conservator would have a background different from that of a taxidermist; an educator's preparation would differ from that of an exhibit designer's.

In addition, different museums often look for different qualifications. Some prefer candidates to have an advanced degree or certificate in museology (museum studies). Others expect to hire professionals with strong academic concentrations in, for example, art history, history, or anthropology. Most are impressed with a combination of academic and hands-on training earned through internships or volunteer programs.

Is a Career in Museums Right for You?

In spite of the diversity of museum careers, there are several skills and personal traits common to all museum professionals. For a start, all museum workers need excellent interpersonal skills. Educators, tour guides, and exhibit designers present information to staff and visitors; directors and curators supervise staff and cultivate contacts with donors and other community members; interpreters, security guards, and museum gift shop staff constantly interact with visitors; museum support staff must deal with each other; and so on. The ability to get along with others and to work well as part of a team is a vital asset in museum work.

Of equal importance is the ability to communicate through the written word. Museums meet their missions with their collections of objects, but in order to do so, museum workers must have strong writing skills. Good written language skills show themselves in grant applications, exhibit catalogs, brochures, administrative and scholarly reports, training and educational materials, legal agreements, interpretive labeling for exhibits, object records, and many other documents.

Other personal characteristics and abilities are also crucial. Before pursuing formal training leading to a career in museum work, it would be a good idea to look at the following checklist and see how many of the qualities apply to you. Although many of these qualities are natural skills, many can also be learned.

People skills
Speaking and writing skills
Business skills
Computer skills
Manual dexterity
Imagination

Creativity
Curiosity
Resourcefulness
Commitment to education
Patience
Flexibility
Problem-solving ability
Ability to handle multiple tasks
An understanding of the mission of museums and how it is
achieved

Training Options

How you proceed will depend on your interests and circumstances.
If you are clear from the start about what avenue you wish to pursue, you can tailor a course of study at the university of your choos-
ing. The courses you take or the degree toward which you work
will depend in part on whether you are a new student or are already
a museum professional making a midcareer change.

Traditionally, new hires to the field of museum work have completed a bachelor's and master's degree in academic disciplines
appropriate to the intended career. Curators for art museums have
studied art and art history; curators for natural history museums
have studied biology, anthropology, archaeology, and so forth.
Although such a background still serves as the main foundation for
successful museum work, for the last thirty years or so, more and
more people have explored university programs offering practical
and theoretical training in the area of museum studies. Courses on
museum management, curatorship, fund-raising, exhibit development, and law and museums offer a more specific approach to the
work at hand. Coupled with a broad background in the liberal arts

or specialization in an academic discipline, this course work provides the museum professional with a knowledge base better designed to serve the needs of the museum.

Whatever you choose to study, most museums require an upper-level degree, either in an academic discipline or in museum studies, museum science, or museology. An intensive internship or record of long-term volunteer work is also required.

Described here are three possible tracks that a student might pursue to prepare for a career in museums. Note that track three is for the museum professional changing careers or upgrading skills.

Track One
- Bachelor's degree in general museum studies, museology, or museum science
- Master's degree or doctorate in a specific academic discipline
- Internship arranged through the university or directly with a museum in a particular field

Track Two
- Bachelor's degree in liberal arts or a specific academic discipline
- Master's degree or certificate in museum studies, museology, or museum science
- Internship arranged through the university or directly with a museum in a particular field

Track Three
- Master's degree or certificate in museum studies, or
- Non-credit-bearing certificate in museum studies (short-term course)

The internship is considered the most crucial practical learning experience and is generally a requirement in all programs. The internship can run from ten weeks to a year with varying time commitments per week.

Evaluating the Options

The American Association of Museums (AAM) publishes three resources that provide essential information for students considering a career in museum work.

1. *Careers in Museums: A Variety of Vocations Resource Report* offers information on career planning. The book explains the world of museum work and professional opportunities in museums. It includes suggested educational qualifications and experience for specific positions, information on how to obtain an internship, definitions of museum terms, a list of job placement resources, and an annotated bibliography.
2. *Museum Studies Programs Guide to Evaluation Resource Report* allows prospective students to conduct their own individually tailored analysis of how well a museum studies program will meet their particular needs.
3. *Graduate Training in Museum Studies: What Students Need to Know* covers such topics as how to decide between a certificate and a master's degree; finding an internship to suit your particular needs; and the practical value of a museum studies degree in today's world.

These as well as other useful publications are available through the AAM bookstore; see Appendix A for contact information.

Volunteering and Internships

Although formal academic training is vital to your résumé, hands-on experience is of equal importance. Not only does it provide a host of significant skills, it also helps you to make an informed decision about the suitability of museum work. If you start with a term of volunteer work, even before beginning a college program, you will have a better idea of what career options museums have to offer and whether these options are right for you.

Many museums rely heavily on volunteer energy and can place volunteers in almost every department, from tour guide and gift shop sales to assisting curators and exhibit designers.

The easiest way to volunteer your time is to contact the museum's volunteer coordinator, who will work with you to match your interests with the museum's needs. Volunteer programs are usually flexible about the number of hours and days per week expected of volunteers.

Most academic museum studies programs require an internship before a degree or certificate can be awarded. In addition, many museums have their own internship programs that are offered to full-time students as well as recent graduates. You can check first with your university department staff to see what arrangements are traditionally made. If the burden is on you to arrange an internship, either during your academic program or after you have graduated, contact the museum's internship coordinator. If the museum has no formal internship program, talk first to a museum staff member to determine where there might be a need. Then you can write a proposal incorporating your interests in a department where help will be appreciated.

Internships can be either paid or unpaid and are usually a more formal arrangement than volunteering. The number of hours and weeks will be structured, and the intern might be expected to complete a specific project during his or her time at the museum. Often college credit can be given.

The AAM has published a resource report called *Standards and Guidelines for Museum Internships*. It covers what museums expect from their interns and what interns can and should expect from the museum. It is available through AAM's bookstore, whose address is given in Appendix A.

Later, when it comes time to look for a job, a successful internship or stint of volunteer work can open the door at the training institution or at other museums.

Turn to Chapter 7 to learn more about volunteering and to meet the volunteer coordinator at the Museum of Science, Boston.

3

Art Museums and Galleries

Not surprisingly, most people who work in art museums and galleries are art lovers. And not only do art lovers keep museums functioning today, they are the reason art museums started in the first place. Most of the famous art museums around the world acquired their exhibits from private art collectors, whether through voluntary donations or as the result of political changes.

Historically, the principle of public control over art and art collections was firmly established in France during the Revolution, when the royal collection was nationalized in 1793 and opened to the public as the Louvre Museum.

In the late 1700s and early 1800s more and more privately owned collections became available for public view, such as those held by King Frederick William III of Prussia, leading to the establishment of the Kaiser Friedrich Museum in Berlin, and the tsar's private art collection, forming the exhibits at the Hermitage Museum in Saint Petersburg, Russia.

The National Collection of Fine Arts in Washington, DC, was established in 1846 as part of the Smithsonian Institution; in 1906 it was designated a national gallery of art. The museum was then renamed the National Museum of American Art in 1980.

Types of Art Museums

Art museums can be classified into two major categories: private museums, under the authority of a board of trustees composed of private citizens and a director chosen by the board; and public museums, administered directly by national or local government.

In addition, art museums fall into two basic types: the general museum, presenting a broad range of works from early times to the present, and museums that specialize in one particular era, artist, region, or type of art.

Aesthetics Versus Economics

In recent years, costs for building maintenance, staff, utilities, and insurance have escalated, while federal funding has decreased. How art museums support themselves has become a controversial issue. Once free to the public, many museums now charge admission. Membership subscriptions are aggressively sought as another major source of revenue. Most public museums also solicit donations from individuals and businesses and vie for corporate and government grants. These practices, while both legal and ethical, affect a museum's choices by forcing it to give precedence to those exhibitions and acquisitions that can be funded by outside sources.

In other words, the art you see displayed in a museum might not have been chosen for its aesthetic value alone, but for its ability to, at least in part, raise income. Exhibitions with mass appeal are most likely to find financial sponsorship; art that is less familiar to the general public is correspondingly less likely to be funded.

This cold reality often creates a dilemma for a museum's director and acquisitions curator. However, most museum professionals stand by their objectivity, despite having to frequently defend their independent position in spite of the preferences of patrons.

Job Titles in Art Museums

In the past, art museums functioned mainly as storehouses for objects, but in recent years their role has been greatly expanded. More and more large art museums try to serve the interests of the community in which they are located. In addition to exhibiting their own collections, many museums develop special "traveling" exhibitions that are loaned out to other institutions for display. They also conduct tours of their collections, publish catalogs and books, provide lectures and other educational programs, and offer art classes.

With all these varied roles, art museums can now offer a wealth of employment opportunities to job seekers. As discussed in Chapter 1, many of the same job titles are found in different types of museums, although the training, specific duties, and working environments of the professionals holding these job titles will vary. A conservator working in a natural history museum, for example, will be concerned with a variety of objects and materials; a conservator in an art museum will mostly handle paintings or ceramics.

Art Museum Curator

Curators in art museums are responsible for the preservation of the collection and for implementing its visual accessibility to the public. The curator is usually an art historian knowledgeable about the physical properties of handmade objects. Although curators have a general background in the history of art, they usually specialize in a particular area. Large museums that have diversified collections employ several curators for the different departments such as American, European, modern, Oriental, primitive, decorative arts, or photography.

Curators oversee the collection and participate in obtaining new acquisitions. They also verify the authenticity of a painting or object by researching its provenance, a document attesting to the work's previous owners and exhibitors.

The curator also supervises the installation of the museum's permanent collection. He or she determines the number of objects to be exhibited and decides when they will be shown. Working with the exhibit designer, the curator also plans how objects or paintings will be displayed.

Associate curators and/or curatorial assistants report directly to the curator and help with the varied tasks the profession demands.

Museum of Fine Arts, Boston

The Museum of Fine Arts, Boston, is in its 135th year. The museum houses collections of more than one million objects from all over the world. With more than seven hundred employees, the Museum of Fine Arts has an extensive job roster. Here is a list of the main departments, each with its own staff of workers:

Curatorial staff—manages the collections
Development office—handles fund-raising
Financial office—processes everything from art works to office supplies
Registrar's office—tracks the collections

Library—is one of the largest museum libraries in the
country, with an extensive collection of books on art
that is open to the public

Education department—hosts concerts, lectures, films,
and gallery talks and presents programs to over fifty-five
thousand schoolchildren a year as well as to adults

Legal office—handles legal issues

Restaurant staff—operates three dining facilities

Museum shop—sells books, posters, and other specialty
items

Public relations and marketing department—deals with
the press and local, national, and international tourism
offices

Publications department—produces pamphlets,
brochures, art books, and catalogs

An Assistant Curator of Paintings

Erica Hirshler works at the Museum of Fine Arts. She began as a
volunteer at the museum in 1983. Only four months later she was
offered a paying, part-time job, which two years later developed
into a full-time position as assistant curator. Hirshler earned her
B.A. from Wellesley College in art history and medieval studies in
1979, her M.A. in art history from Boston University in 1983, and
a museum studies diploma from BU the same year. In January 1992
she earned her Ph.D. in art history, also from Boston University.

Duties of an Assistant Curator

Hirshler talks about her job as assistant curator for a collection of
two thousand paintings. The departmental structure includes the
curator, an associate curator, an assistant curator, and four research

assistants and fellows with various areas of specialization. As assistant curator, Hirshler handles a wide range of duties, including working on the permanent collection; organizing special exhibits; conducting research; writing catalogs, art books, and copy for exhibition brochures; administering loan requests; and arranging for the display of various items in the galleries. She also responds to a large amount of correspondence, answering inquiries that range from a private citizen curious about the history of a family-owned painting to a scholar needing information for a project at another institution. As Hirshler sums up her work routine, "There is no typical day. It's a very seat-of-the-pants type of schedule."

Hirshler describes what she likes about the job. "I like working with the objects. It's a special thrill working with the real thing that you don't get from slides. I'm interested in them as physical objects. You gather them together for a special exhibition; you get to really examine them." The downside is that a busy schedule leaves little time to do everything she would like to do. As she says, "There's a lot of paperwork. It would be nice if there were less paperwork and more time to work on scholarly things. Research is important."

Of course, it's every assistant curator's hope to move up the curatorial ladder, working toward the additional money and prestige that accompany a promotion. In many cases, a curator would have to be willing to change locations to move ahead. But opportunities can be limited, and sometimes it's better to stay right where you are.

Hirshler explains the situation: "We have one of the two best collections of American paintings in the country—the Metropolitan Museum of Art in New York City has the other—so you balance the strength of being in an institution that values your field against some of the other things that might not be so positive. In other words, moving to a weaker collection to get a better title. It wouldn't be worth it."

In Hirshler's opinion, moving to a smaller museum with a smaller collection is not advisable unless one is interested in working toward a career as director. A director of a small museum could eventually move to a directorship at a larger museum. However, this career track is more administrative and provides little opportunity for scholarly work.

The salary is not high, but like most museum professionals, Hirshler is not in this for the money. "I could be doing lots of different things for $30,000 a year," she says. "I really love what I do or I wouldn't be doing it." According to the U.S. Bureau of Labor Statistics, in 2002 median annual earnings of curators in museums were $33,720.

Advice from Erica Hirshler

Hirshler stresses the need for flexibility in this job, since projects often come up that require workers to juggle several things simultaneously. As she says, "You'll have a couple of different exhibitions you're working on at the same time. One might be coming along in two years, one might be coming in two months. And you go back and forth between them. Or you'll have three different catalog deadlines for three different shows. You have to write your manuscript and turn it in to the editor. You might get to do a book every five years."

In Chapter 4 you will meet a curator at the Smithsonian's National Museum of American History.

Public Relations Professional

Public relations professionals in a museum setting work primarily with the press to promote and publicize the museum's activities, exhibitions, and special events.

A Public Relations Coordinator

As public relations coordinator at the Museum of Fine Arts, Judy Negip is the museum's media contact. In her work she focuses on promoting special exhibitions and the museum's various educational programs for local, national, and international media.

Negip attended Simmons College in Boston and earned her B.A. in communications in 1992. She served an internship at *Boston Magazine*, where she was hired upon graduation. While working with the staff of the Museum of Fine Arts public relations department on a project for the magazine, Negip learned about an entry-level position in the department. She applied, was hired, and later was promoted.

Working in a museum wasn't actually Negip's first career choice. She says, "Although I had no objection to it, I'd had no particular interest in working for a nonprofit. I'd been thinking more of crisis PR, product PR, and that's what I had focused on more in my studies—issues such as the Tylenol poisoning scare and that type of thing.

"But working here has been interesting because you find out that your skills in PR aren't necessarily related to the product. It's how effective or persuasive you are in any setting. I didn't know a great deal about art. Now, I certainly know an incredible amount, but that wasn't necessary to get the job."

Duties of a Public Relations Coordinator

Negip's main responsibilities are preparing press releases and press kit materials, which include glossy flyers for the exhibitions. She writes the text, prepares the object list, and makes the wall text accessible to the press.

Negip is also a liaison between the press and the museum staff. She handles all requests for interviews, setting up schedules and alerting staff. She also determines whether requested interview topics are appropriate for public knowledge. For instance, although the press is often interested in how the museum protects its collections, matters of security are not discussed so as to prevent a security breach. Such situations emphasize the need for diplomacy in public relations work. As Negip says, "People can be rather persistent when they want to know something, and you don't want to offend anyone, but you have to protect the museum's interests first. You need to be creative dealing with them; you need to give them something else or offer them something more."

The aspect of her work that Negip enjoys most is the constant contact with the press and the public. "I enjoy letting people know what the museum has to offer. It's rewarding to deliver the message to people that we're not a stodgy institution with paintings on the walls—that we're dynamic, and that it's always exciting inside."

Although Negip finds her work challenging, she also admits that sometimes the challenges can be frustrating. Trying to get the press to cover a specific item, or coverage being bumped in favor of other news, is always a source of frustration for a public relations professional. On the positive side, Negip doesn't need to make a lot of cold calls to have a story picked up. Three or four months before an event or exhibition opening she issues a press release, and this is usually enough to get calls coming in as the event gets closer.

The reputation of the museum also helps in Negip's job. As she says, "We're one of the top five museums in the country, and the museum attracts its own press audience. People are very in tune with what's going on at the museum, and they want to cover it. And because we're a tourist attraction for Boston, the Boston press and calendar editors feel a need to let the public know about museum events. We work well together because we need each other. We want to be in the paper as often as we are and the paper needs to cover what we're doing because it has a public to satisfy."

Salaries in the PR Office

According to the National Association of Colleges and Employers, the average entry-level salary for public relations positions in non-profit settings in 2004 was $27,750. A coordinator could earn in the mid to upper thirties. The director's salary would be $60,000 or more, depending on location and experience.

"The salary would be much more lucrative working in other than a nonprofit setting," Negip explains, "In private industry I'd be earning in the high thirties or forties, but the money isn't what you're after. You refocus after you've found your niche. When you're studying, you hope that the earning potential will be vast, but once you find what you truly enjoy, it becomes less and less important."

Advice from Judy Negip

Negip's advice is to enter the field in any position available to get your foot in the door. Keep an open mind and be ready to assume any responsibility given to you. The knowledge you acquire and your familiarity with the museum will become a great asset, which is proven by the fact that many people working in museums have advanced from a variety of job titles and levels.

The skills you'll need to succeed in public relations, in addition to the obvious written and oral ones, are patience, flexibility, and a sunny disposition. "Your people skills need to be a cut above the norm," says Negip. "When handling press people and the general public, you need to be able to extend yourself and be even overaccommodating. But sometimes that's hard to do, because you don't always come in with the same mood every day.

"You might spend 90 percent of your day on the telephone, and there needs to be a certain rapport. Even when it doesn't seem fair—yesterday they [news media] didn't run your story and they're not going to, but then they call you for fifteen other things they need immediately—you still have to be cheerful and say, 'Okay, I'll get this to you right away.' It's a quality many people don't possess."

Registrar

Registrars keep track of every item in an art museum's collection. Paintings and other art objects are often moved to different areas within a museum or are transported to other museums for exhibition, making it necessary to maintain accurate files. Registrars are also responsible for shipping objects and obtaining insurance.

Registrar's Office at the Metropolitan Museum of Art, New York City

Although a small museum might have only one registrar, a large museum such as the Metropolitan Museum of Art in New York City needs a much bigger staff to cover all the responsibilities of an expansive and active collection.

In addition to the head registrar, the Metropolitan has four people handling exhibits, two working with outgoing museum loans, one dealing with loans to the museum and exams (items brought in for review), a storeroom manager, one conservator and one assistant to the conservator (in addition to the many conservators working in the conservation department), and four packers.

The rankings for registrars at the Metropolitan Museum of Art are as follows:

Assistant registrar
Senior assistant registrar
Associate registrar
Head registrar

An Associate Registrar

Aileen Chuk worked for eleven years at the Museum of Modern Art in New York City before coming to the Metropolitan in 1994. She has a bachelor's degree in art history from Fordham University in New York and currently serves a dual role as administrative manager and associate registrar.

Duties of an Associate Registrar

As administrative manager, Chuk works with the head registrar, taking care of all personnel issues and supervising the work of junior staff members. Here she tells us about her role as associate registrar.

"A registrar's duties vary depending on the size of the museum. At the Metropolitan, once a curator decides what will be in a particular show, the registrar receives a list of the items (sometimes two hundred objects) and begins to make all necessary arrangements. Many of the registrar's duties involve shipping artworks, which includes packing, arranging transportation, scheduling couriers, securing insurance, and keeping an archive of all works that are lent to or borrowed from the museum. The eighteen curatorial departments of the museum maintain their own storage rooms and control their own inventories, but the registrars perform annual inventory spot-checks within those departments to ascertain that their records are correct.

"I love my work," Chuk says. "It's varied and interesting. For instance, you may be dealing with very small impressionist paintings on one exhibition, and then you may be dealing with massive, several-thousand-pound twentieth-century sculptures for the next exhibition. Each show you do provides you with a whole new set of challenges."

Chuk describes one particular challenge that she faced. Charged with collecting an oversized painting from a home in Omaha, Chuk had to figure out how to move a painting that was larger than the doorway. She had to arrange for the painting to be taken off its stretcher, brought outside, put back on the stretcher, packed into a crate, and put on a truck. And all of this coordination was done long distance. Chuk had to find people who were familiar with artwork and capable of handling such a task to ensure that the piece would not be damaged in transit. She contacted local museums and was referred to someone with the expertise to manage the move. Chuk says that it often takes years of experience to be able to coordinate such a project.

Along with such challenging responsibilities come some negatives. Chuk explains that the work of a registrar involves a good deal of overtime and often can take away from personal and family time. Shipments sometimes arrive in the middle of the night, and works that are being loaned to other institutions must be escorted to their destinations. As Chuk says, "Sometimes you want to do it, and then it's a real plus to the job, but sometimes you don't. You might have just come back from vacation, or you'll be missing your daughter's piano recital, or you have a lot of work piling up that you need to get to.

"But, I've been almost everywhere. Last year I went to Germany, France, Italy, and Switzerland five times. I went to Japan twice a couple of years ago. It can be very rewarding and lots of fun, but sometimes the demands are such that you're trying to do an enormous amount of work in your office and prepare for a courier trip at the same time."

Salaries can be another downside. "Museum work can be extremely rewarding, but it's not a career suited for someone who is interested in making a lot of money," Chuk explains.

Overall, however, Chuk finds much more positive than negative about her work. She enjoys working on a project from inception to completion and being part of the overall effort that makes a major exhibition possible.

Registrars work as part of a team. While the curatorial departments generally work within their own areas, the registrars get to interact with the staff of all of the departments. At the Metropolitan, Chuk works with eighteen different types of art and with people who have a variety of different specialties. As she describes her role, "You're the central core for all the flow and traffic in and out of the building."

Advice from Aileen Chuk

Given her experience as a museum registrar, Chuk can offer some insight into what it takes to be successful in this career. A registrar should be very detail oriented and have excellent organizational skills and a good memory. These skills help when one is juggling two hundred artworks and must keep track of all details and lender requirements for each piece. Although everything is documented, Chuk finds that she also commits the information to memory.

A background in art is not absolutely essential to working as a registrar, but Chuk advises that it is definitely helpful. In her experience, registrars are interested in art and are either artists them-selves or have some basic artistic skills. Most will have a bachelor's degree in art history. Chuk recommends having at least a prelimi-nary degree in the arts so that you can gain some familiarity with the field. In addition, museum studies programs grant certificates in museum administration, and this is a very helpful course to pur-sue after gaining a bachelor's degree. The Metropolitan takes many interns from such programs.

In addition to education, much of a registrar's work is learned on the job. Chuk says, "There are a number of different specialties within the registrar's office, and the more senior you get, the more complex work you're assigned. As you gain experience, you tend to do exhibitions rather than museum loans or other various tasks that might be in the department. It usually starts at something quite low. If you started with exhibitions, you'd usually start with very small shows. Normally people work their way up the ranks, starting with exams, then work to loans, then go to exhibitions."

Collections Manager

The collections manager supervises, numbers, catalogs, and stores the art specimens within each division of the museum. An under-graduate degree in the area of the museum's specialization is the minimum requirement. An advanced degree in museum studies with a concentration in a specific discipline is recommended.

A collections manager must have knowledge of information management techniques and the ability to accurately identify objects within the museum's collection. Knowledge of security practices and environmental controls is also important.

In Chapter 7 you will meet a collections manager at the Museum of Science and Industry in Chicago.

Art Conservator

Many people think that a valuable object is safe once it is housed in a museum; unfortunately, it decays on the museum's walls or shelves just as fast as it would decay on yours. Many different conditions contribute to that decaying process: light, variations in humidity and temperature, pollutants, pests, and accidental damage.

Conservators (who were formerly called art restorers) concern themselves with preventing that decay. They help prevent deterioration through a number of steps:

1. Examination of the object to determine its nature, properties, method of manufacture, and the causes of deterioration
2. Scientific analysis and research on the objects to identify methods and materials
3. Documentation of the condition of the object before, during, and after treatment and to record actual treatment methods
4. Preventive measures to minimize further damage (such as providing a controlled environment)
5. Treatment to stabilize objects or slow their deterioration
6. Restoration, when necessary, to bring an object closer to its original appearance

Training for Conservators

Conservators are a group of highly trained professionals who have gone through a number of steps to gain their expertise. Training programs are few, and as a result, they are very competitive.

According to the American Institute for Conservation of Historic and Artistic Works, a conservator must have the following:

- Appreciation and respect for cultural property of all kinds—its historic and sociological significance, its aesthetic qualities, and the technology of its production
- Aptitude for scientific and technical subjects
- Patience for meticulous and tedious work
- Good manual dexterity and color vision
- Intelligence and sensitivity for making sound judgments
- Ability to communicate effectively

During the course of a training program, student conservators are exposed to working with a variety of materials before going on to specialize in a particular area. They learn skills to prevent the deterioration of paintings, paper and books, fiber, textiles, ceramics, wood, furniture, and other objects. There are even conservators in architectural conservation and library and archives conservation.

Training most traditionally is gained through a graduate academic program, which takes from two to four years. Apprenticeships or internships are a vital part of training and are usually taken during the final year of study. Some programs might offer internships that run concurrently with classes.

Admission requirements for the various graduate programs differ, but all of the programs require academic prerequisites, including courses in chemistry, art history, studio art, anthropology, and archaeology.

Some graduate programs prefer their candidates to have a strong background in conservation, which can be gained through undergraduate apprenticeships and fieldwork in private, regional, or institutional conservation laboratories.

A personal interview is also usually a requirement of the application process. A candidate's portfolio must demonstrate manual dexterity as well as familiarity with materials and techniques.

Careful planning at the undergraduate level will help improve your chances of acceptance into a graduate program, but because acceptance is very competitive, it is not unusual to have to repeat the application process. However, before reapplying, it is a good idea to enhance your standing by undertaking additional studies or fieldwork. Many programs, on request, will review your résumé and suggest avenues for further study.

Conservation Degree and Internship Training Programs

The names and addresses of the thirteen conservation degree and internship training programs currently active in North America are listed in Appendix B. Contact those that interest you for their specific admission requirements.

In Chapter 6 you will meet an object conservator at the Carnegie Museum of Natural History.

Development Officer

Most museums depend on donations, membership fees, and grants for their funding; consequently the development office is a vital organ in any museum. A development officer is responsible for fund-raising activities, including conducting membership drives, planning and implementing special fund-raising events, and pursuing grants and donations.

To qualify for a position as a development officer, you must have good people skills, good organizational skills, and you must be able to work as part of a team.

To pull together all the elements of a successful fund-raising campaign, development offices rely heavily on the help of their volunteer staff. Having experience as a volunteer in this department, as in any other museum department, is a great way to get your foot in the door.

Photographer

Many art museums will keep a professional photographer on staff to provide photographic documentation of the various fine arts collections. The photographer would also oversee the photography of general museum events and activities and would be responsible for studio and darkroom facilities as well as personnel issues for his or her assistants.

Many photographers are self-taught; others receive their training in a variety of ways, such as through traditional art schools, through university art and photography departments, and through apprenticeships.

A portfolio documenting your professional experience would be a requirement for employment.

Photographers also find work in planetariums (see Chapter 8) and other types of museums, such as those highlighted throughout this book.

Librarian

Most mid- to large-size museums maintain extensive libraries that are open to the public. The collections they handle generally relate to the museum's content; in other words, an art museum will carry art books, a science museum science books, and so on. And just as in any public library, a museum library needs a professional staff to carry out its operations.

The head librarian, who is usually assisted by one or more associate or assistant librarians, is responsible for acquiring library materials; maintaining the catalogs and inventory of publications, reference materials, and periodicals; responding to public inquiries; and providing reference and research materials to museum staff.

Museum librarians need the same educational preparation as librarians in other public or private facilities. Usually the minimum requirement is a master's in library science (M.L.S.).

Marketing Director

A marketing director can be found in most large museums, though many institutions combine the marketing department with the public relations or the publications department. The marketing director can work as part of a team or as a consultant to other museum departments and volunteer groups to promote specific events, activities, products, or services.

The general responsibility of the marketing director is to coordinate the museum's advertising programs, getting the word out about programs, events, and products for sale.

A degree in marketing or communications would be the basic requirement for entry into this field.

Tour Guide/Docent

Although most museums rely on volunteer help to act as tour guides and docents (the two job titles have essentially the same meaning), there are still a few spots for paid professionals. Most tour guides have a college degree in either education or the field of study the particular museum encompasses.

In Chapter 4 you will meet a tour guide for the museums under the auspices of the Nantucket Historical Association.

Art Gallery Positions

Art galleries operate in a very different manner from art museums. Whereas a museum depends on membership and grants to support it, an art gallery must earn its keep by selling works of art to the public.

Some art galleries are small with only one or two employees in addition to the director/owner. Large galleries, especially those in New York, maintain a staff of ten to twenty people, most of whom would carry the title of assistant director.

Director/Owner

The owner of an art gallery is responsible for every aspect of running the gallery, from selecting which artists to exhibit to designing the layout of the show, hanging the artwork, promoting the show and the gallery, and selling to clients.

Assistant Director

A large gallery could have ten or so assistant directors. These individuals work directly with the owner, representing the gallery and reflecting the owner's taste. Assistant directors work with customers, or clients as they are frequently called, discussing the artwork and making sales.

Packager/Maintenance Personnel

Most large galleries have "backroom staff," personnel responsible for packaging purchased pieces of art for shipping and maintenance workers who, under the direction of the director or an assistant director, hang the paintings in designated positions.

In many cases, packagers or maintenance personnel are artists who take a menial job in a gallery to allow them to continue to be able to paint and to be involved in some level in the art world. It is also a good way for a future assistant director to get a foot in the door. It puts you in contact with the art arena, allowing you an opportunity to learn. You will learn why the gallery is showing a particular artist's work, how it is exhibiting this work, and what is being done to publicize the show. It is always worthwhile to know every aspect of the business, and these so-called menial jobs are very important.

Framer

Most small galleries farm out their work to frame shops, but the larger galleries often employ a framer who is skilled in cutting mats for prints and cutting frames for canvases. However, most artists deliver their work to galleries already framed, so the need for professional framers hired directly by a gallery is small.

Receptionist

Many large galleries, especially those in New York, hire receptionists to greet customers and answer questions over the phone. They must be knowledgeable about the artwork shown and be able to intelligently discuss different aspects of the work. Most receptionists have a degree in art; many use the position as a stepping-stone to assistant director.

A Gallery Owner

Matthew Carone is the owner and operator of the Carone Gallery, a prestigious establishment in Fort Lauderdale, Florida. He handles mainly contemporary art; American, some European, and some Latin American paintings; and sculpture. He is also an established painter himself, and he is often invited to show his work at other galleries.

The Carone Gallery is a family business that has been in existence since 1957. Carone is the owner and his wife is his partner. His son was assistant director until he left to work for the local symphony. Carone, who is semiretired, divides his time between Florida and Lenox, Massachusetts, where he also has a studio.

The busy season in south Florida occurs during the winter, when tourists are more likely to take advantage of the warm climate. Experience has taught Carone that the summer months are not very lucrative, so he closes the gallery for five or six months until the winter season begins and people are again ready to buy art.

Carone has some options for acquiring artwork. Because of his experience and reputation, artists want to show their work at his gallery. While this allows him to be selective, Carone stresses that this is not generally an option for those just starting out. At the beginning, a gallery owner must trust his or her own taste and try to find undiscovered talent.

It is important for an owner to establish that his or her gallery is a serious establishment. In Carone's case, this happened by way of graphics by the masters. He began working with original prints by Picasso, Cezanne, and Matisse and soon built a reputation as a serious dealer of high-quality art. This made it easier for him to work one-on-one with important artists.

Since many of the sources for these prints are based in Europe, Carone traveled there every couple of months to meet with dealers to discuss current events in the art world. He had discovered a counterfeit Picasso print, and this added to his reputation and generated a lot of publicity for his gallery.

Carone describes what happened: "I'm color-blind, but I have become value sensitive. I can see the value of a color, the lightness or darkness, more than a person with normal color vision. The ink used for this Picasso was called an ivory black, which is the blackest of blacks, but I knew that the originals had a warmer black. On the basis of that, I knew there was something wrong, so I went to Paris and showed it to a very important Picasso dealer."

The dealer confirmed that the print was a fake, which brought Carone to Picasso's biggest dealer, who decided that the print must be shown to Picasso himself. The artist returned the print with the word *faux* written across it, and his signature. In this unusual way, a counterfeit print gained some value, since it was signed by Picasso. As Carone says, "The fake was terrific. The FBI, of course, got involved with this; they had an idea who he was, but it was never pursued because it's very difficult to prove. They never found out."

Running an Art Gallery

At the Carone Gallery, a day at work is generally a very pleasant experience. During the high season, January through March, Carone begins his day by looking over his show before greeting his first client. Once a client arrives, the two might spend a social hour drinking coffee and discussing the works on exhibit. With luck, the conversation will escalate to the point where the client picks up on Carone's enthusiasm and decides to make a purchase.

In addition to clients, Carone talks with artists who want to show their work at his gallery. They send slides for his consideration and schedule appointments to discuss the possibility of showing at the gallery. Carone never refuses to talk with an artist, since this is one way in which he might decide what to show.

Even if a talented artist presents beautiful work, Carone must make an educated decision about pursuing the show. Whether the art will sell is of prime importance. As Carone says, "Each space on the wall costs you a certain amount of money. You have to make your expenses, and every inch of wall space must try to pay for itself."

Once a show is selected, Carone begins working on the installation. This involves deciding where each painting will be hung in relation to other works. In Carone's experience, hanging the art is something that one acquires a feeling for over time. As he explains, "It's very important to be able to hang an artist next to someone he's compatible with. You don't want any conflicts in image. You wouldn't want to put an ethereal kind of painting next to a very guttural abstract. You could destroy that very sensitive painting if it's within the view of something incompatible. You learn this on the job and through discussion, and it's a gut feeling. There's no one book that can describe this. There is a sense that one feels."

Once a show is running, Carone begins thinking about the next one. He generally runs a show for three weeks and then takes one week off before the next. He normally does four shows in a season. After the shows are over, he displays his own inventory, which includes items that he owns and has accumulated over the years.

To summarize his experience, Carone says, "It's been the most wonderful life for me. I can't tell you how great it's been. First of all I'm a painter, but I also play the violin, and I use my gallery for concerts. I come to work thinking 'I'm coming home. I'm going to where I want to be.' I love the artists, I love selling important stuff, I love people responding to my enthusiasm. It's been glorious. I'm a very lucky guy—I love what I do."

Art Gallery Earnings

Most galleries work on a 50–50 percentage basis with the artist. However, if the artist is very popular, the gallery might get only 30 percent. Of course, the more popular the artist, the greater the attraction, and the more business there is for the gallery. As for actual prices, Carone has displayed artwork ranging from $2,000 for a small wooden mask to $9,500 for a painting. He has sold art for $43,000, and has shown items even more expensive than that.

Getting Your Foot in the Gallery Door

Carone points out that it can be difficult even to get an interview in a large gallery. In light of this, he never refuses to talk with anyone who aspires to work in art and is happy to let people pick his brain about the profession. Carone suggests that anyone interested in pursuing a career in an art gallery should talk with an established gallery owner to get a feel for the business.

Carone points out that managing and owning a gallery is hard work and that many new ventures fail. He suggests having as many contacts as possible before starting out and recommends talking with museum curators and directors as well as other gallery owners. Schedule an informal interview, and try to get an honest picture of what the profession is really like.

An assistant director should be well versed in art history, which is helpful in describing the influences of contemporary artists. While a degree in art is certainly beneficial, it is not a requirement. In fact, Carone does not have an art degree.

Overall presence is important for working in an art gallery. Assistant directors and directors should be extroverted without being pushy, and they should be articulate about their subject. Carone sums up his view of the skills needed to pursue this work: "Sales skills can be learned, but you must have a sincerity about the work. I've always felt that you never sell a painting, you sell yourself first. That's really a barometer for selling. And if I really love something, it's the easiest thing in the world for me to sell, because if my clients pick up on my enthusiasm, they're sold. Consumers are, in most cases, not really sure of their taste and if what they like is good. My clients, loyal to me over a period, automatically become an extension of what I feel about art."

Starting a Gallery

A major factor in owning a gallery is finding the right space. Carone believes in looking for space in the best possible location, even though it might be more expensive. The best places are in a cultural area, near a museum, where art is already a focus. Inexpensive space off the beaten track will be harder to promote and might not be successful.

Rent is the main expense for gallery owners, followed by advertising costs, insurance, and utilities. A gallery requires minimal furnishings, mainly a desk and a storeroom. Good lighting is a must.

Of course, deciding what you want to sell is a huge part of starting a new gallery. This is not necessarily easy to determine, since even great art can be difficult to promote. As Carone points out, even Picasso was laughed at early in his career. An owner must be committed to the art he or she wants to sell, and that comes from a sincere love of the work. You must establish a stable of artists who reflect your taste and whose work can help to establish your reputation as a serious gallery.

Carone sums up the risk involved in opening an art gallery. "The tragedy of the arts is that it caters to only 3 percent of the population. Now that could be quite a bit if you're in a cultural area, but that 3 percent is distributed among the arts in general—music and art—so if you want to hone in on just a segment of that, on just painting or just sculpture, there's not that much out there. You're in a minority arena. It's a risky business. But when something happens to have a magic combination, it's good and the public responds to it, that's paradise."

4

HISTORY MUSEUMS

ALTHOUGH THE UNITED STATES might be considered a young country, at least by the rest of the world's standards, it is still a land steeped in history. And nothing makes history come alive more than to hold a piece of it in your hands. Throughout the country there are thousands of history museums, historic houses, and public buildings as well as restored or reconstructed villages—even entire cities—that offer the possibility of employment.

Many are large enterprises that employ scores of professionals to handle their day-to-day operations. In contrast, other museums are small and operate with only a handful of employees and dedicated volunteers.

The larger the museum, the more specialized are an employee's duties. Professionals in midsize or small museums must be willing to take on a variety of tasks. However, knowledge of or familiarity with all areas of museum functions, in addition to a strong background in a particular discipline, are important qualifications for any staff member.

A Firsthand Look at History Museum Careers

One of the best ways to get a feel for what a particular job or job setting would really be like is to talk to someone who works there. In the remainder of this chapter, you'll be given a bird's-eye view of what many consider to be a plum job setting—the Smithsonian Institution. You will also be introduced to a variety of professional museum workers employed there, as well as to a director of a smaller museum.

Profile of the Smithsonian Institution

When most Americans think about spending a day at the mall, they have shopping on their minds. But residents and seasoned visitors to Washington, DC, know that the Mall, located between the U.S. Capitol and Washington Monument, is a manicured strip of land housing the bulk of the museums of the Smithsonian Institution complex. Here is a list of all Smithsonian museums:

Anacostia Museum and Center for African-American
    History and Culture
Arthur M. Sackler Gallery
Arts and Industries Building
Cooper-Hewitt National Design Museum (New York)
Freer Gallery of Art
Hirshhorn Museum and Sculpture Garden
National Air and Space Museum
National Museum of African Art
National Museum of American Art
National Museum of American History, Behring Center
National Museum of the American Indian and Heye
    Center (New York)

National Museum of Natural History
National Portrait Gallery
National Postal Museum
National Zoological Park
Renwick Gallery
Smithsonian Institution Building, the Castle
Steven F. Udvar-Hazy Center (Chantilly, Virginia)

The chief executive officer of the Smithsonian is given the title of secretary. The institution is governed by a board of regents that, by law, is composed of the vice president of the United States, the chief justice of the United States, three members of the Senate, three members of the House of Representatives, and nine private citizen members. Traditionally, the chief justice of the United States has served as chancellor of the museum.

The Castle houses the Smithsonian's central administration offices. Each individual museum has its own director and staff.

Curator at the National Museum of American History

The National Museum of American History, part of the Smithsonian Institution complex on the National Mall, is devoted to the exhibition, care, and study of artifacts that reflect the experience of the American people. The museum has the responsibility for preserving more than sixteen million objects acquired over the last century. It has more than 430 employees on staff and receives in excess of five million visitors a year.

Curators are specialists in a particular academic discipline relevant to a museum's collections. They are generally responsible for the care and interpretation of all objects and specimens on loan or belonging to the museum, and they are fully knowledgeable about each object's history and importance.

Depending on the museum and its area of interest, curators can work with textiles and costumes, paintings, memorabilia, historic structures, crafts, furniture, coins, or a variety of other historically significant items.

Curator of the Twentieth-Century Consumerism and Popular-Culture Exhibit

Charles McGovern is supervisor of the American History Museum's Division of Community Life. In this position he oversees a group of technicians, specialists, collections-based researchers, curators, and other support staff. He is also the curator responsible for the Twentieth-Century Consumerism and Popular-Culture exhibit. This department covers the history of entertainment, leisure, recreation, and commerce.

McGovern graduated from Swarthmore College in Pennsylvania in 1980 with a B.A. with honors in history. He immediately entered graduate school at Harvard and earned his M.A. in history in 1983 and his Ph.D. in American civilization in 1993.

McGovern taught history at Harvard during his graduate studies, and from 1986 through 1987 he was a research fellow at the Smithsonian. In 1988 he returned to the Smithsonian as a full-time curator.

The exhibits that comprise Twentieth-Century Consumerism and Popular Culture are probably the most popular and well-known in the museum. Visitors come to view Judy Garland's ruby slippers from *The Wizard of Oz*, Archie Bunker's well-worn chair, or Julia Childs's kitchen.

McGovern's interest in cultural history began at an early age. He watched a lot of television and listened to the radio and was part of the mass popular culture of the 1960s. His parents told him about the times when they were growing up, sharing with him stories about the early days of radio. When McGovern got to high school and read books his teachers recommended, he realized that Babe Ruth and Laurel and Hardy and the Marx brothers, personalities he cared very deeply about, were as much a part of history as Franklin Delano Roosevelt or World War I.

As a curator, McGovern is a historian who must be able to understand and explain the lives and beliefs of our ancestors. He says that at the Smithsonian, "We try to do that respectfully, understanding the world as they saw it. As we do that, we see how culture reflects the times, the fears, and the ideals and problems of a given society. You cannot look at certain creations of our popular culture without seeing those kinds of elements in them."

McGovern documents the history of the everyday life of American people and is responsible for the creation and maintenance of the collections in his area. His job is divided into three parts: acquisition of new objects and exhibits, exhibiting and interpreting, and research. His primary job duties are to oversee the building collections, develop exhibitions, conduct research, write, speak publicly, and act as graduate advisor to eleven research fellows.

The collections that McGovern is responsible for include a fascinating variety of objects. Among the items in the collections are a hat that Jimmy Durante used in his stage appearances; Howdy Doody; Mr. Moose, Bunny Rabbit, and the Grandfather clock from the "Captain Kangaroo" show; Mister Rogers's sweater; the leather jacket and hat worn by Harrison Ford in the *Indiana Jones* films; the Hawaiian shirt, baseball cap, and ring that Tom Selleck wore in "Magnum, P.I."; old 78 rpm records; movie posters; and comic books.

As curator, McGovern looks for items that provide insight into American consumerism and commerce. The collections include the bonnet worn by the woman who posed for the Sun-Maid raisin box, a huge collection of turn-of-the-century advertising and marketing materials, and a collection of memorabilia from world fairs from 1851 to 1988.

Most of the items in the collections have been donated to the museum. McGovern explains that the museum has a very small budget for acquisitions; it is, therefore, unable to compete with private galleries. As he says, "People must be willing to donate, so we look for people who either don't need the money or get the point of what we're trying to do."

Despite the best intentions, however, not every item that is offered can be accepted. McGovern describes the case of Charlie Chaplin's cane: "Someone called once and wanted to donate Charlie Chaplin's cane. But first, how do I know that it was his cane? It's impossible to document that. And second, Chaplin probably went through thousands of canes. Those bamboo things snapped very easily. Something like that we couldn't take."

This story points to one very important aspect of McGovern's job as curator: the ability to document items. He must be familiar with the history of every object in the collections, and the number of items is staggering. As he says, "It's not as if I were a curator of paintings, where I'm trained in oils and brush techniques. Once in a while I have to confer with an appraiser or dealer to determine authenticity."

Given the size of the collections, it is not possible for all items to be exhibited simultaneously. McGovern explains that less than 2 percent of the collection is on display at any time, and the rest is kept in storage. While some of the most famous items, such as Dorothy's ruby slippers or Archie Bunker's chair, are on permanent display, others rotate.

It is McGovern's responsibility to decide which items are exhibited, stored, and rotated. He must also see that the items are cared for to avoid deterioration. This task requires occasional removal of even the most popular items, a fact that doesn't always please the paying public. McGovern explains that most visitors to the museum expect to see specific items and are disappointed if they are not on exhibit. As he says, "People travel a long way expecting to see a certain item, and if it's not on display they're usually upset. They don't realize that they should check with us first if they're coming to see something in particular. We took Charlie McCarthy off to clean him one day, and within a half an hour we had three phone calls saying where was Charlie McCarthy."

McGovern explains that the exhibiting part of his job is a team effort. As curator, he works with exhibit designers to decide how an item should be displayed. The designer plans the layout of the object and the accompanying text, graphics, and props. The care and maintenance of the item is the responsibility of a conservator, who also determines things such as the maximum amount of light to which an item can be exposed to avoid deterioration.

While the exhibits are the most public part of McGovern's job, he believes that research is actually his primary duty. In his opinion, "All the collecting and exhibiting doesn't mean anything unless you have something to say. You have to figure out first what point you're making. Our point is the showing of everyday life of the American people, and for earlier times, that's something that has to be researched. Of course, you do research to support the things you already have in your collection, but the research also helps you to determine what you should be out there collecting."

The Smithsonian as Training Ground

Every year the Smithsonian awards dozens of research fellowships and provides funding and access to museum collections for Ph.D. candidates.

To be hired as a curator, a candidate must possess or be near completion of a Ph.D. Entry-level positions include technicians and specialists and research-related jobs. Paid internships and volunteer positions are usually available and are a good way to get a foot in the door.

As McGovern points out, jobs for curators at the Smithsonian seldom become available. But because the Smithsonian has a certain reputation and skill in training, it is a good place to gain a foundation and then go out to other areas or institutions for work. An internship at the Smithsonian will go a long way in securing employment elsewhere. He believes that because of the Smithsonian's size, candidates might find working in smaller museums with a more fixed mission to be more interesting as well.

Salaries for Curators

A beginning curator who has almost completed his Ph.D. would draw a salary somewhere in the midthirties. Smithsonian staff are employees of the federal government and follow the GS scale. A high-level position such as a supervisory museum curator, a job that requires specialized experience, could start at more than $100,000.

Exhibit Designer at the National Museum of American History

The exhibit designer, also known as a *preparator*, works closely with curatorial and education personnel to convey ideas into permanent or temporary exhibits. They use drawings, scale models, special lighting, and other techniques in their work. An exhibit designer can have administrative responsibilities and may supervise the production of exhibits.

Many small and even midsize institutions do not have room in their budgets for a specialist exhibit designer. In such a situation, one or two people such as the director or curator might perform the design functions in addition to the duties of their own specialty. Or, in some cases, the museum will contract with an outside firm for exhibit design work.

The Smithsonian Institution is a large operation and employs more than twenty exhibit designers and assistants; five of those designers work specifically for the National Museum of American History.

Senior Exhibit Designer

Hank Grasso is a senior exhibit designer working in all of the different departments of the National Museum of American History. He is also the owner of Hank Grasso Planning and Design, Inc., based in Kensington, Maryland.

Grasso attended Denison University, a small liberal arts school in Ohio, before transferring to Penn State and studying in the wood products division; he specialized in wood as an art medium, looking at both its aesthetic and structural uses. He combined his study of wood products with courses in architecture, including drafting and drawing, and graduated in 1976 with a B.A. in interdisciplinary studies. He later attended Pratt Institute in New York, where he took graduate courses to increase his conceptualization skills and learn more about different fabricating techniques.

Between his time at Penn State and Pratt, Grasso worked for a couple of different private design firms that were contracted by various museums. While building up his portfolio, Grasso had an opportunity to work on exhibit design for the John F. Kennedy Library in Boston; the Basketball Hall of Fame in Springfield, Massachusetts; the Bowling Hall of Fame in St. Louis, Missouri; the New York Historical Society; the United Nations; the Metropolitan Museum of Art; the Frederick Douglas Place in Baltimore; and the Buffalo Bill Historical Center in Cody, Wyoming.

Grasso came to the Smithsonian in 1990 as a visual information specialist, the government's position title for an exhibit designer. He generally functions as part of a team of professionals including curators, collections managers, conservators, scriptwriters, audience advocates—or educators as they are more commonly known—and project managers.

He came on board specifically to work with the American Encounters Show, the museum's Columbus quincentenary presentation, dealing with five hundred years of history in America. He has also worked on the designs for "Working People of Philadelphia" in the Life in America exhibit; Science in American Life; the East Broadtop Railroad; Manufactured Weather; and Feed Bags as Fashion (see the "Close-Up" later in this chapter).

Grasso discusses the process of exhibit design: "If you have a thousand images and ten square feet of space, you need to come up with a vehicle that will allow those images to be displayed. You can compress them into a videodisk or a series of slide presentations or storyboards. We look at the information we're wanting to convey and then translate it visually, keeping an eye to special allocations."

Exhibit designers generally follow one of two distinct models. The first is the traditional model, whereby staff members perform very specific duties and rarely stray from their designated jobs. For instance, the curator passes his or her abstract ideas over to the designer, who then translates them into a physical presentation. The curator is responsible for content and ideas and the written word; the designer is responsible for the environment and the aesthetics and graphic design.

The second is the collaborative exhibition development model. In this more modern model, a team of professionals work together to produce a design. One of the Smithsonian's permanent exhibits, the American Encounters Show, was designed using this model. As Grasso explains, "We created design tools so all parts of the team could understand each other. We could look over each other's shoulders and know what we were seeing."

The Exhibit Design Process

Designing an exhibit is clearly a very involved process. Following are just a few of the many steps a collaborative team follows when working on a new exhibit.

1. Listen to ideas and identify interpretive goals: Why are we telling this story? What is the most important message we want to convey?
2. Look at the available space and create a floor plan.
3. Combine steps 1 and 2 by prioritizing ideas and looking at the elements that will hold the exhibit together.
4. Decide how the exhibit will come about: presentation vehicles, techniques, and technology.
5. Choose the objects and images that will best tell the story.
6. Make a scale model rendering all the individual objects and labels and graphic images.
7. Translate design control drawings (sets of drawings that have to do with the general contracting and building of spaces and with the making of exhibit parts).

8. Write the script and labels for the exhibit.
9. Begin the competitive bid process for general contracting.
10. Construct a full-scale model.
11. Conduct audience research: How does the audience react? Can viewers understand the material and the ideas being presented?
12. Complete construction.
13. Generate promotional and outreach elements.

Educational Options for Exhibit Designers

Today there are three main educational preparation choices for someone wishing to pursue a career as an exhibit designer. Institutions such as Pratt or Parsons School of Design offer good courses in industrial, graphic, and commercial design. Some universities can provide a liberal arts education combined with certain skill courses. Or a candidate can attend a professional program in a field such as architecture.

Grasso suggests that once you complete your theoretical education, so much more of what is still out there to study can be learned through internships and working for diverse design firms. This also gives the new exhibit designer a chance to build up a portfolio, an important tool for moving on to the next position.

Salaries for Exhibit Designers

Exhibit designers work either in museums or for private firms on contract with museums. Not surprisingly, salaries paid by the private sector often top those a museum can pay, even if the designer is doing the same work in the same institution.

Salaries for entry-level workers can begin in the low to midtwenties and are a few thousand per year higher in a private firm. An exhibit designer with more than ten years of experience could expect to earn somewhere in the forties. According to the National Association of Colleges and Employers, in 2002 the average starting salary in museums for undergraduate degrees in design and graphic arts was $30,093.

A Student Intern's Journal

In addition to his duties as exhibit designer, Grasso is often responsible for the supervision of interns. Kendra Lambert from Auburn University in Alabama spent her last summer in college learning about graphic design at the National Museum of American History. Following are some highlights excerpted from Lambert's journal. Read them to see if a career in exhibit design might interest you.

- Attended staff meetings with curators, designers, educators, and the team writer
- Helped build prototypes of pueblo and Spanish missions used in the exhibit, using PageMaker program on a Macintosh computer
- Learned to draw objects to scale
- Designed title logo for the exhibit
- Worked in the exhibit production lab, setting type for labels, observing silk-screening process, and positioning text on panels
- Attended exhibit opening and answered questions from the press

Lambert explains in her own words what she learned from her student intern experience: "I have learned that designing exhibits requires a person who is flexible to schedule the meetings that are a part of working in a team and still complete the required drawing and model work.

"It is important for an exhibit designer to make an exhibit more accessible to the public so viewers can begin to learn what ideas the curators are attempting to communicate. I've observed that exhibit designers need a graphic artist to make decisions about type treatment, type placement, logo development, and creating graphics.

"One of my goals this summer was to arrange portfolio reviews in the Washington, DC, area and meet professional designers. Hank [Grasso] looked at my design portfolio and immediately recommended I speak with a colleague. This interview taught me a lot! I also had the opportunity to meet with the former director of design at the museum. I am scheduling an appointment with the assistant of exhibition design at the National Gallery. I have recorded suggestions from these reviews that will enable me to improve my portfolio and decide on a direction for my senior project. It has been valuable also in developing interviewing skills. I feel more confident about my work and have a clearer idea of what aspect of design I will follow as a career as a result of this internship."

Lambert graduated from Auburn University and is now working at the Birmingham Museum of Art as a publications designer. She designs all the printed promotional pieces that the museum uses, such as invitations, newsletters, posters, and T-shirts. She is in the process of applying to graduate school to study for a master of fine arts in design history, with the ultimate goal of becoming a freelance designer. Lambert also hopes to teach design at a university.

Close-Up of an Exhibit: Feed Bags as Fashion

Do you remember poodle skirts, off-the-shoulder sweatshirts, leg warmers, and safety pins? All were flash-in-the-pan fashion statements, meant to be fun and frivolous, with no more staying power than an ice-cream cone on a hot summer's day.

The Feed Bags as Fashion exhibit, which was held at the National Museum of American History in 1991, detailed a unique time in American history when necessity was truly the mother of invention. Depression-era women in the 1930s turned what started out as a survival mechanism into a fashion trend that lasted more than thirty years. In the process, they created a positive effect on the economy and influenced big business in a way no one could have imagined.

Because money was scarce, and what there was of it had to be spent on essentials such as food and medicine, there was none left over for clothing. Rural farm women began saving the bags that feed came in to create clothing from them.

But these were not fashion-senseless women. Although they had to use very raw materials, they worked hard and took pride in what they produced to outfit their families.

Most bags were made of a cotton cloth known as *sheeting*, and before the 1940s, manufacturers emblazoned their logos and brand names across the bags in stubborn ink. Consequently, the bags had to be scrubbed, bleached, beaten, and rinsed to make cloth that could begin to approach being appropriate for clothing.

The cloth was then dyed or embroidered, and with a few snips and a few handy stitches here and there, the shapeless feed bags were soon converted into fashionable dresses, nightgowns, children's garments, and underwear. The feed-bag cloth was even used for quilts, curtains, and tea towels.

The practice spread throughout rural communities across the country. When the feed-bag manufacturers heard about it, they decided to take action. They didn't condemn the practice or raise the prices of the feed or charge additional fees for the bags. They cleverly saw a marketing opportunity and in 1941 began imprinting the bags with colorful solids and fashionable patterns. The ink logos were transferred to paper labels or bands.

Women began to control what kinds of feed were bought to collect the bags they would need to finish a set of outfits. Feed manufacturers began to use specific prints on their bags to identify their product or company.

"Years ago," a feed merchant in 1948 complained, "they used to ask for all sorts of feeds, special brands, you know. Now they come over and ask me if I have an egg mash in a flowered percale. It ain't natural."

Two trade associations, the National Cotton Council and the Textile Bag Manufacturers Association, began national advertising campaigns that lasted from 1940 until 1964. They distributed instruction booklets that taught women how to sew with feed bags and sponsored national sewing contests and fashion shows. Two major manufacturers of clothing patterns, McCalls and Simplicity, developed patterns to the specific sizes of feed bags.

Enterprising women with surplus bags began a lively trade selling to neighbors and pocketing the profits. Arthur Fleming, a retired poultry farmer from Georgia, recalled his wife's expanding business. "What she didn't want she would sell. . . . There were people who came around and bought those sacks. . . . If I'm not mistaken, the sacks was bringing back then about from twenty to twenty-five cents apiece. Yeah, my wife'd save up a hundred or two hundred . . . and she'd sell 'em."

Even though most of us were probably unaware of the feed-bag clothing trend, we can see how it would merit a place in a museum of American history. Given the longevity of the trend and how it impacted the industry and the public, it seems an appropriate exhibit to teach us about a little-known part of our country's past.

Director of a Small Museum in Nauvoo, Illinois

A museum director must have specialized knowledge of the museum's collections and be responsible for acquisitions, preservation, research, and presentation. A director must also be familiar with policy issues, handling funding and budgets, supervising staff, and coordinating museum activities.

Nauvoo, Illinois, is a historic city on the banks of the Mississippi River near the point where Iowa, Missouri, and Illinois meet. Fairly isolated, Nauvoo is 260 miles south of Chicago and about 170 miles north of St. Louis.

The city was originally a Sac and Fox Indian village, named Quashquema for their chief. When Mormon church founder Joseph Smith arrived in 1839, he renamed the site Nauvoo, from the old Hebrew word meaning "beautiful place."

The town is laid out like a mini-Williamsburg, with beautiful gardens and more than two dozen restored homes and shops open to the public. Early crafts have been given a second life, and skilled artisans give daily demonstrations. Most of the staff, including the director, the guides, and caretakers, live on-site. In fact, the year-round population of Nauvoo numbers only eleven hundred, and most of these residents work for one of the two main churches that share ownership of the town.

The Church of Jesus Christ of Latter-Day Saints, whose headquarters is located in Salt Lake City, Utah, owns and operates the visitors center on the north side of town as well as many neighboring properties.

The Joseph Smith Historic Center, on the south side of town, is operated by the Reorganized Church of Jesus Christ of Latter-Day Saints. A visitors center houses a greeting gallery, two theaters, and a small museum room displaying artifacts of the Smith family.

There is also a library containing rare books of the period along with reference books on the restoration and reconstruction of historic buildings and artifacts.

Visitors to the Joseph Smith Historic Center also tour the Joseph Smith Homestead, which includes a log cabin portion that was built around 1803, the 1842 Mansion House, the Smith family cemetery, and the Joseph Smith Red Brick Store, a building that was reconstructed in 1979.

Don Albro is the director of historic sites at the Joseph Smith Historic Center. He feels he was chosen for this position because of his long relationship with the church (he has been an ordained minister since 1955), his interest and studies in history, and his management skills gained while in charge of an extensive sales force in private industry.

As director, Albro is responsible for a full-time secretary, two maintenance workers, eight student interns, and ten volunteer senior guides. He coordinates the student intern program and volunteer guide staff and their training, and oversees the historic properties' upkeep, maintenance, and reconstruction. As director of a small museum, Albro performs functions that would not normally fall under the director's realm in a larger organization. A typical day for him might also include the following tasks, which he admits are his favorites:

- Conducting a tour
- Assisting with cooking demonstrations at the site's summer kitchen
- Working in the gift shop or in the Red Brick Store
- Repairing buildings
- Trimming trees, planting flowers, weeding and cutting grass (all thirty-four acres of it)

Tour Guide with the Nantucket Historical Association

The Nantucket Historical Association maintains twenty-three properties, eight of which are open to the public. Other than the Whaling Museum, most of the properties are historic houses.

Jeremy Slavitz is curator of the Nantucket Life-Saving Museum. Here, however, he talks about the experience he had as a paid docent for the Nantucket Historical Association. Although he grew up in a location noted for its historical significance, it was not until Slavitz attended college that his interest in history developed. Unsure of what he wanted to do, he enrolled in a variety of classes. The history courses interested him the most, and he discovered it was important to work in a discipline he enjoyed. Slavitz graduated from the University of Massachusetts, Amherst, with a bachelor's degree in history and a specialty in naval history. He plans to go on to complete a graduate degree. The summer after graduation was his first season as a docent.

What Slavitz enjoyed most about his job as a docent was the ability to work with history without working solely in research. He was able to interact with people and even realized that he might enjoy a career teaching history. In describing this work, Slavitz says, "I gave information every day and struggled to make it interesting. I enjoyed the challenge."

The docents work in pairs. There are college students and older residents, which makes the job interesting. Docents alternate taking guests through the museum and are especially busy on rainy days, when visitors to the island prefer to explore indoors.

The docents with the Historical Association try to portray the history found in the museums. They strive to give visitors a complete picture of the people who lived through various time periods and the different ways the buildings and objects were used. As an example of this, Slavitz cites Nantucket's Oldest House. Built in 1686 by wealthy businessman Jethro Coffin, it is the most prestigious house on the island. The docents show the house as it was during Coffin's lifetime and also as it was during the eighteenth century, when it was purchased by a new owner. As the island's population grew, the house was considered modest in size and lost a good deal of its initial prestige. The docents also show the house as it is today, a small structure with only five rooms.

The docents follow a general guideline but are free to tailor their presentations based on their visitors. Slavitz describes a somewhat unique experience he had one summer: "There was a local boy whose parents were members of the Historical Association. They gave him their pass, which allows admission to about twelve different properties, put him on his bicycle, and sent him on his way. The boy would bring his friends, and over the course of the summer, he followed me around to the different sites where I worked. He'd wait until most of the other visitors had left, so I could show him parts of the buildings he would find the most interesting. The kids peered up chimneys and climbed through root cellars and figured out how the loom worked. They had a great time. Someone else would have an entirely different interest, so I would focus on another aspect for them."

Training for Nantucket Historical Association Docents

The Historical Association provides a book about each museum that includes all the known information about the house or building. New docents learn the information in these books, as well as learning oral history from more experienced docents. Slavitz found the training process very enjoyable. As he says, "We're learning from people who have learned from people before them. Some of the older docents have lived on the island all of their lives, and they can pass down the history, as well as their own experiences with the property."

Hours and Earnings for Tour Guides

Since his pay as a docent was only $6.00 an hour, Slavitz put in as many hours as possible and generally worked a forty-hour week spread over six days. Because one of the museums is open at night, he was also on duty for some evening hours.

5

LIVING HISTORY MUSEUMS

LIVING HISTORY MUSEUMS offer a range of opportunities for people with special interests above and beyond a love of museums. Here are some skills and personality traits common to many living history professionals:

- Theater skills (with a touch of the ham)
- Research skills (with an interest in a particular period in history)
- Skill working with your hands (for costume designers, craftspeople, artisans, and landscapers)
- Ability to pay attention to detail

A Firsthand Look at Living History Museums

The following is a list of job categories found in living history museums; those marked with an asterisk (*) are explored in this chapter:

Archaeologists

Architectural conservators*

Architectural historians*

Artisans/craftspeople (coopers, potters, silversmiths, woodworkers, and so on)*

Business affairs directors

Character interpreters*

Collections managers

Costume designers*

Curators

Development and membership directors

Educational programs directors

Gardeners and groundskeepers*

Historic interiors designers*

Landscape archaeologists*

Landscape architects*

Personnel managers

Presenters*

Public relations coordinators

Researchers*

Restoration architects*

Salespeople

Security personnel

Topiary gardeners*

Visitor services coordinators

Once you step through the gates of a living history museum, you leave the present behind. In this chapter, we take a look at some of the positions available at Colonial Williamsburg and Plimoth Plantation, two well-known living history museums.

Overview of Colonial Williamsburg

Visitors to Colonial Williamsburg meet historical figures, witness events, and participate in the daily lives of the people who helped bring about American independence.

For eighty-one years, from 1699 to 1780, Williamsburg was the thriving capital of Virginia, one of the original thirteen colonies. After the American Revolution, when the capital was moved to Richmond, Williamsburg began a decline that lasted 146 years. It became a sleepy Southern town with crumbling roads and buildings, overgrown gardens, and only a distant memory of patriots and prosperity.

In 1926, with his love of American history and a belief that anything is possible, John D. Rockefeller Jr. began the Colonial Williamsburg restoration project to return this once-important city to its former glory.

Now, after nearly eighty years of work, eighty-eight original eighteenth- and early-nineteenth-century structures have been restored, and more than five hundred others have been reconstructed on original foundations. None of this could have occurred without extensive archaeological and historical investigation.

The principal thoroughfare in Williamsburg is the Duke of Gloucester Street, which began as nothing more than a winding horse path flanked by a tavern and a few shops and houses. Then in 1693, with the establishment of the College of William and Mary (America's second-oldest university, with Harvard being the first) at the western end and the impressive Capitol building at the far eastern end, the street was widened and became the busy center of daily activity. Today it is closed to traffic, though an occasional horse-drawn carriage or stagecoach clatters by. Eighteenth-century shops and houses still stand, shaded by beautiful old trees lining the hard-packed dirt walkways.

But these buildings are not just empty symbols of a bygone era. Many of the homes shelter permanent residents or employees of the Colonial Williamsburg Foundation, or they act as inns to house the many visitors who come every year. Those buildings that are open to the public are filled with the same artifacts, activities—and people—that made up daily life in colonial times.

Overview of Plimoth Plantation

Plimoth Plantation is a living history museum that has re-created the year 1627, seven years after the arrival of the *Mayflower* at Plymouth Rock.

At Plimoth Plantation you can listen to seventeenth-century Goodwife Cook plan her day or share tidbits of gossip with Governor Bradford's sister-in-law. John Alden is there, making barrels in his one-room cottage or helping other villagers erect a new house. Not too far away, seventeenth-century sailors swab the decks or repair the lines on the *Mayflower II*, while passengers discuss their worries about surviving the first winter in the New World.

Character interpreters at Plimoth Plantation attend to all the necessary tasks to keep the village thriving. They work in the fields, care for the farm animals (which have been "back-bred" to resemble breeds from three hundred years ago), and build new houses or repair existing ones.

Character Interpreter

The most visible living history museum employees are the men and women decked out in authentic period costumes. They can be found waiting inside the buildings or walking through the grounds, and although they might seem to be there just for decoration or photo opportunities with tourists, most are trained researchers, actors, and presenters. A select group of these staff members use first-person interpretation or role-playing to explain their characters' place in history. They are called *character interpreters* or *people of the past*. In actuality they are skilled social historians who have researched and assumed the role of specific early residents.

In Colonial Williamsburg, for example, you can follow Mrs. Powell about town as this eighteenth-century housewife does her errands, or visit the Powell House and speak with the character interpreter who portrays Mr. Powell, the prominent Williamsburg builder.

You can spend an afternoon in the Capitol yard listening to colonial gentlemen discussing events of the day or converse with Mr. Samuel Henley, an eighteenth-century professor at the College of William and Mary, and learn about the values and traditions of his time. You can even eavesdrop on young gentlemen as they prepare for college and share their expectations and concerns for the future.

Children can join a costumed interpreter to explore the interaction of colonial family life, youth apprenticeships, education, work, and leisure time.

Adam Waterford, a free black cooper, and young Charles, the son of the Powell family's cook, are also on hand for a glimpse into the colonial African-American experience.

A Character Interpreter at Colonial Williamsburg

Jeremy Fried is the head of character interpreters at Williamsburg. For more than ten years, he has also been interpreting the role of James Hubard, a colonial lawyer.

Fried describes his job: "My character spends most of his time in chambers, a fair-sized room in the courthouse, with a table in the middle seating twelve people. I sit down with a law book and quill and paper, and people come in and chat. But I don't work from a prepared script; that's what makes this form of interpretation different from other forms of living history."

Fried explains that a character interpreter works with the help of the museum's research staff to uncover the life of an eighteenth-century person. Information is gathered from any available documents, including personal letters, newspaper, and so forth. These sources allow the researchers to make inferences about the person's life and beliefs and to portray their ideas, social knowledge, and political opinions as accurately as possible.

Visitors ask "James" questions about his life and work, such as why he became a lawyer and what his family is like. Sometimes visitors are so intrigued that they stay for quite a while, making it a challenge for Fried to stay in character throughout the conversation.

Qualifications

For the position of character interpreter, Colonial Williamsburg seeks individuals with acting ability and the attributes that go along with it. Fried stresses that the most important qualifications an applicant should possess are the ability to communicate with people, a pleasing personality, and an inquisitive mind. These requirements generally hold true for all living history museums, regardless of location. At Williamsburg, knowledge of colonial Virginia history, experience in character interpretation, and a degree in acting are all considered advantages. Certain positions require an audition. In addition, candidates would have to be age- and sex-appropriate for a particular character they might be asked to play.

Fried adds that while the museum prefers to hire those who have majored in history, this alone is not enough preparation for the job. As he says, regardless of your educational background, you will have to research the specific time period covered by the museum.

"We have a number of folks with history degrees, but we also have a retired florist and a former petty officer in the navy," Fried says. "It's a mixed bag of backgrounds. I have a degree in theater from the American Academy of Dramatic Arts in New York."

Fried points out one other qualification: "An applicant would have to be willing to accept a pretty low pay range."

Hours and Earnings for Character Interpreters

Most full-time employees put in an eight-hour day for a total of forty hours per week, including weekends and holidays. At least four hours each day are spent in the characters' natural environment—in chambers, in class at the college, in their shops or homes. The rest of the time is spent moving around town, chatting with visitors.

Ample time during the week is also allocated for research or to produce facsimile newspapers in the winter months.

A full-time entry-level character interpreter earns between $8.30 and $16.50 an hour, depending on the position. But although it's an hourly wage, employees are given full benefits. Most contracts are for a ten-month period. A percentage of employees are laid off for two months during the winter and then are rehired when the high season starts again.

Offsetting the low salaries, Fried points out, is that the people really enjoy working for the foundation. "It's a nice work environment. The biggest stress is being hospitable to folks on vacation. And that's not a bad situation."

Of course, salaries vary from one living history museum to another, but they generally follow the same range offered in Williamsburg.

Advancement

Occasionally there are opportunities for character interpreters to move into more administrative roles. The National Association for Interpretation offers certification in historical interpretation to those who pass an exam and have experience. It offers conferences and workshops, as does the Association for Living History, Farm, and Agricultural Museums. Contact information for both societies is given in Appendix A.

How to Apply

The Colonial Williamsburg website offers detailed information about available jobs and how to apply. For complete information visit www.history.org/foundation/human_resources.

Costumer

Most living history museums employ professional costumers to keep their character interpreters and presenters outfitted in authentic period clothing. Costumers generally work behind the scenes reproducing the apparel the average inhabitant would have worn.

A Costumer at Plimoth Plantation

Patricia Baker is a wardrobe and textiles manager at Plimoth Plantation. She graduated from the Massachusetts College of Art in

1976 with a B.F.A. (bachelor of fine arts) degree in crafts. Her concentration was in fabrics and fibers.

Baker began working at Plimoth Plantation as a character interpreter immediately after graduation. In 1985 she joined the wardrobe department and became manager the following year. Her office and work space occupy a section of a converted dairy barn on the grounds of the museum. The atmosphere is that of a cozy living room with lots of shelves and fabrics draped here and there, sewing machines and rocking chairs, a large cutting table, garment racks, and a radio.

Baker's department makes clothing that is representative of what the middle class would have worn in 1627. In an attempt at true authenticity, the costumers provide interpreters with enough clothing to dress authentically right down to their undergarments.

The basic undergarment for both men and women is a linen shift that falls to the knees. Over that the men wear breeches and a doublet, which is a close-fitting jacket that comes to just above the waist. The breeches are tied into the jacket with laces. Women wear a plain corset over their shifts, and this is followed by a number of petticoats and skirts as well as a padded roll to enhance their hips.

Since the costumers try to duplicate the materials used in the seventeenth century, the garments are made of wool, linen, and cotton, all naturally dyed. Much of the sewing is done by hand, as it would have been in the 1600s.

The costume department also makes the household furnishings that are used in the various exhibits. Items on display include the seventeenth-century versions of objects such as sheets, pillowcases, feather and straw beds, paneled bed curtains, tablecloths, napkins, and cupboard cloths.

Maintaining and repairing existing costumes and furnishings is also part of the costumers' responsibilities, as well as conducting the necessary research to keep their creations accurate for the particular time period. Because there are so few surviving garments, the costumers look to different sources such as paintings, engravings, woodcuts, written descriptions, wills, inventories, diaries, and plays. They also study the few remaining garments on display in different museums through Plimoth Plantation's extensive slide collection of styles and techniques.

Job Outlook and Earnings

The wardrobe department at Plimoth Plantation is a small one, currently employing only four workers. Other larger living history museums, such as Colonial Williamsburg, need more people. A good way to get a foot in the door is to apply for an apprenticeship, internship, or work-study position.

A new graduate just starting out could expect a starting salary around the midtwenties, depending on the location and available funding.

Artisan

Most living history museums employ skilled artisans to demonstrate early crafts and trades. Some of these artisans perform in the first person, playing the role of a particular character of the time. Others wear twentieth-century clothing and discuss their craft from a modern perspective.

In the stores and workshops lining the Duke of Gloucester and Francis Streets in Colonial Williamsburg, you'll find harness makers, milliners, tailors, needleworkers, silversmiths, apothecaries, candle makers, bookbinders, printers, and wig makers. In the Pilgrim Village and Crafts Center at Plimoth Plantation are coopers, blacksmiths, joiners (cabinetmakers), potters, basket makers, and weavers.

In addition to demonstrations, artisans often produce many of the items used on display in the various exhibits. These include the furniture, cookware, and even sometimes the actual buildings.

Interpretive Artisans at Plimoth Plantation

Most of the items the Pilgrims used in 1627 were either brought with them on the *Mayflower* or imported later. Because the Pilgrim Village at Plimoth Plantation is time-specific to the year 1627, only those crafts that were practiced at that time are demonstrated. In addition to their principal occupation as farmers, 1627 Pilgrims were coopers, blacksmiths, thatchers, and house builders. The interpretive artisans perform in costume and play the role of a designated Pilgrim documented to have lived in Plymouth during that year.

A Cooper at Plimoth Plantation

Tom Gerhardt interprets the character of one of the most famous Pilgrims, John Alden, a cooper who worked both inside a one-room cottage he shared with his wife and two children and in the adjoining yard. As a cooper, Gerhardt makes barrels and other wooden containers, such as buckets and churns, while answering visitors' questions about life in seventeenth-century Plymouth.

Gerhardt explains that although in Europe people still practice the cooper's craft as it once was done, there are only a few barrel makers working in this country today. Wooden barrels are made mostly for the wine and spirits industry, but now it's a mechanized craft using power tools and machinery. The finished product is the same as the old craft, but the method is different. Coopers at Plimoth practice the craft as it was done in the 1600s, using only hand tools.

In addition to his duties as an interpretive cooper, Gerhardt is also responsible for general woodworking. He is one of several Pilgrims building a new house on the grounds.

"What I enjoy most about Plimoth Plantation is that there are a number of very creative and talented people here," Gerhardt says. "If you're willing to do the work, you can learn a good deal for yourself, while at the same time you're educating the visitors.

"There are so many people who will help you; you can be inspired by what they're doing. And you have the time to explore and develop your skills."

Gerhardt's interest in history began when he was a young child. His father was a volunteer in charge of a small museum in Virginia, and family vacations were spent traveling around the country visiting other museums. It was on one of these trips that Gerhardt first discovered Plimoth Plantation.

Later he took a few courses under a master cooper in Portsmouth, New Hampshire, and went to college for a couple of years studying general liberal arts and theater. He worked in the technical end of theater for a while but decided he wanted a change. Since he had always been interested in the re-creation of history, in 1985 he came back to Plimoth Plantation and applied for a job as an interpreter.

Crafts Center at Plimoth Plantation

Plimoth Plantation also operates a crafts center where several other seventeenth-century crafts are demonstrated. Potters, joiners, basket makers, weavers, and a gift shop share space in a converted carriage house. Artisans in the crafts center wear twentieth-century clothing and discuss their work from a modern viewpoint.

A Joiner in the Crafts Center

Joel Pontz is the supervisor of all interpretive artisans at Plimoth Plantation as well as a character interpreter for the farmer John Adams. In addition to these, he demonstrates his joinery skills in the crafts center.

Pontz describes his job as stepping back and forth between the seventeenth and twentieth centuries. Several days a week he works in costume in the village as John Adams, picking vegetables or building small animal shelters or fences. On the other days he is in modern clothing in the crafts center demonstrating joinery.

"Joiners were the principal furniture makers of the period, in the age before cabinetry," Pontz explains. "We use different kinds of saws and edged hand tools such as axes, planes, gimlets, and augers, rather than power tools. If we want to reproduce the right texture or style, we have to be purists about it.

"In the craft center, in front of the public or behind the scenes, we make furniture for the village: large cupboards, bedsteads, chairs, mousetraps, and children's toys. We don't want to demonstrate any crafts in the village section of the museum that weren't practiced at the time. It would be anachronistic."

Pontz grew up nearby and started at Plimoth Plantation as a volunteer Pilgrim after school and on weekends. In 1973 he became a full-time interpreter. He learned his joinery skill on-site from the other staff members and the research department.

"I hated woodworking in school," Pontz admits. "It wasn't until I started working at the plantation using hand tools and trying to decipher how things were made that it became interesting for me.

The historical aspect of it was what fascinated me. If it were just doing straight carpentry, I probably wouldn't have stayed with it."

A Potter in the Crafts Center

In the crafts center at Plimoth Plantation, four different potters demonstrate the art of seventeenth-century throwing techniques, though only one potter is on duty at a time. They also make all the pieces that are used in the village by the interpreters. During the winter months when the museum is closed to visitors, the potters make enough items to replenish their stock.

In addition to her own home studio, where she teaches pottery classes, does commission work, and makes pieces for display at various galleries, Deb Mason spends two eight-hour days a week in the crafts center and is the supervisor of the other potters.

Mason explains that since pottery was not made in the village in 1627, the potters do not thereby have to work strictly within the parameters of the seventeenth century. This gives the potters an advantage over the character interpreters. The interpreters have to speak as though they are Pilgrims, and they cannot share any knowledge beyond what would have been known in 1627. Potters in the craft center, however, can answer questions that the interpreters cannot.

The potters use modern equipment, but are considering going back in time and using wood-burning stoves and kick wheels. The electric wheels they use now might make throwing look faster and easier than it was in the seventeenth century, but the techniques are still very much the same.

"The difference is we have to make only period pieces, and there some of the difficulties come in," Mason says. "For example, we're trying to find the right clay bodies to work with. We have a few original pieces on display to study, and you can see the clay color and texture. We've been experimenting, trying to develop clay bodies that are close to the original.

"That's been fairly successful, but we're having a tough time with glazes. They used a lot of lead back then. In fact, almost every glaze was lead based. Because we sell the pieces we make in the gift shop and they're also used in the village every day, we've been trying to get away from lead. It's hard to come up with glazes that have the same shine and the same colors; lead has a very typical look. We're using a ground glass that melts at a low temperature, which is a characteristic of lead and produces similar results."

The potters make ointment pots that hold salves and healing lotions, apothecary jars, bowls, porringers for porridge, oil lamps, candlesticks, and *pipkins*—small cooking pots with a side handle and three little legs on the bottom. They also make three-handled cups, because the Pilgrims often shared their eating implements. The novelty of such items makes them popular in the gift shop.

Mason explains that pottery was hastily thrown in the seventeenth century, since the Pilgrims strove to create utilitarian items rather than objects of beauty. For this reason, Mason says, "My biggest problem is remembering not to throw too well. The advantage to that, though, for potters wanting to work here, is that a high degree of skill is not necessary."

Mason earned her B.A. in art with a major in ceramics in 1973 from Bennington College in Vermont. She taught ceramics full-time for thirteen years at a private school and was the head of the art department her last few years there. She joined the staff at Plimoth Plantation in 1992.

Preparation for Working in the Historic Trades

Pontz advises taking a few courses in historic trades or historic preservation. "But," he cautions, "the skills we need are particular to Plimoth Plantation. Outside courses would be painted with a broad brush, but what's done at Plimoth Plantation is very focused on a particular group of people in a very short time span.

"The best qualification would be a lot of hand-tool work. The tools haven't changed that much over the centuries. Try taking a tree and make a table or a chair from it. That's the best way to learn the art."

Because of limited budgets and a low turnover, openings at Plimoth Plantation are rare. However, interns are occasionally taken on, and there is a volunteer program that could help you get your foot in the door.

Salaries for Craftspeople

Salaries for craftspeople differ depending on whether they are full-time or part-time. The latter group earns an hourly wage ranging between $7.50 and $10.00.

Researcher

Researchers are the backbone behind every living history museum. Without their efforts, the ability to re-create authentic period characters, to accurately restore historic buildings, or to reproduce a facsimile of daily life would be an impossible task.

Director of Research at Plimoth Plantation

Plimoth Plantation consists of four sites: the 1627 Pilgrim Village, the *Mayflower II*, Hobbamock's Wampanoag Indian Homesite, and the Carriage House Crafts Center.

Duties of a Director of Research

Carolyn Travers is director of research at Plimoth Plantation, and it is her responsibility to ensure that every aspect of each program is researched to present as authentic a picture as possible of life in the seventeenth century. Travers might research anything, as she says, "from what was the period attitude toward toads, how a character felt about being her husband's third wife, or the correct way to cook a particular dish, to some obscure point of Calvinist theology."

Research generally includes the life and genealogical background of a character. According to Travers, it is more difficult to research the female characters because there is less documented information available about them than about the males. The researchers use several sources, including court records as well as genealogical research done by professionals from such organizations as the General Society of Mayflower Descendants or writers for genealogy periodicals.

Other types of research are handled by different departments. For example, re-creating authentic buildings and structures is the responsibility of the curatorial department.

Travers attended Earlham College, a small Quaker school in Richmond, Indiana, where she earned a bachelor's degree in fine arts with a concentration in history. She went on to Simmons Graduate School of Library and Information Science in Boston and graduated with a master's degree in library and information science with a concentration in research methods.

Advice from Carolyn Travers

Travers warns that researching is a competitive field and that an advanced degree is needed, specifically in history or library science with a concentration in research methods.

A candidate is not expected to have a general body of knowledge about the specific time period, but he or she must have strong research skills, talent, and experience.

Earnings

New graduates might begin with a salary in the low twenties. As Travers stresses, "You don't do it for the money. There are a lot of psychological payments. One of the satisfactions for me is to be able to change someone's mind about the stereotypes surrounding early colonists."

Landscape Preservationist

Historic landscape preservation is a field of growing interest throughout the country among managers of historic buildings and living history museums. In fact, Colonial Williamsburg is one of the largest employers of landscape architects, designers, and related groundskeeping professionals.

Landscape Architecture at Colonial Williamsburg

Kent Brinkley is a landscape architect in the landscape and facilities services department at the Colonial Williamsburg Foundation. He is also a Fellow of the American Society of Landscape Architects, past president of the Virginia chapter, and coauthor with Gordon W. Chappell of the bestselling book, *The Gardens of Colonial Williamsburg*.

Duties of a Landscape Architect

Brinkley's job includes several different responsibilities. He creates designs for new work that is being planned and is also responsible for maintaining the existing gardens planted years ago by his predecessors. After extensive research and investigation into the landscapes of colonial times, the gardens at Colonial Williamsburg were planted with flowers and plants appropriate to the period. Brinkley makes sure that these plants continue to thrive and selects replacements for any that are no longer healthy.

Brinkley works closely with the director of landscape services, providing the design plans that will be implemented by the landscape services staff. He also gives lectures and tours to groups and garden clubs and occasionally conducts public garden tours to keep in touch with the foundation's visitors.

In addition to his work as a landscape architect, Brinkley is a garden historian. He has a background in history and has conducted research into the development of historical landscapes. He has visited England many times to study country estates and gardens, since English landscape design served as the model for many colonial gardens in the eighteenth century.

Garden history is a fairly new field, but one that could be a specialty for someone interested in both landscape design and history. A combination of history courses would be the right path for someone who wants to pursue this field.

Brinkley also works in the growing field of landscape archaeology. As he defines it, "The purpose is to recover enough evidence to re-create a garden that existed on the site in a given historical period. Landscape archaeology uses traditional archaeological technique to recover fence lines, planting beds, and other evidence."

Brinkley works with archaeologists when they excavate a site at Williamsburg because they may uncover evidence of the original gardens. It is hoped that an excavation will reveal information about pathways, fence lines, and post holes, as well as planting beds and outbuilding foundations. Sometimes actual seed materials are found in excavated planting beds, and laboratory analysis can reveal what type of plant the seed is from.

Brinkley has a B.A. in history from Mary Baldwin College in Staunton, Virginia. He describes his start in landscape architecture in this way: "I'm a dying breed—you see it less and less. But I came to landscape architecture through the back door. Just as lawyers used to be able to read the law under a licensed practitioner and then sit for the bar exam, years ago you used to be able to apprentice in a landscape architecture office under a licensed practitioner. It was an equal-time commitment. In other words, when you got a five-year B.L.A. degree, you generally had to work in an office three years before you could sit for the exam. Or in lieu of that, you could do eight years in an office and then take the exam. I waited ten years before I took the exam.

"I started as a draftsman and worked my way up to vice president of the firm before coming to Williamsburg.

"When I got my job at Williamsburg, I was ecstatic. This was the perfect marriage of my love of history and my work as a landscape architect. It's been wonderful to be able to take two major interests and combine them in a way that allows me to do both."

Advice from Kent Brinkley

Based on his years of experience in the field, Brinkley offers some advice for future landscape architects. Students who are mechanically inclined and curious about how things work are well suited to landscape architecture. There is a lot of drafting involved; you must cultivate your drawing talent to have an edge on the competition.

Good communication skills are important because you might have to present your designs to a group of people. Some sales ability is a plus, since you have to market yourself, your firm, and the design. You would never be wasting your time by taking additional English or drawing classes.

It's a good idea to work in several different offices and get different kinds of experience for the first five or six years after graduation. Some people study landscape architecture but don't know which aspect to pursue; they need time to test the waters before knowing where their niche will be.

Anyone entering this field should work for two or three years before taking the licensing exam. "It's comprehensive in scope and tests you on a variety of things. You need some experience under your belt before you tackle it," Brinkley says.

In conclusion, Brinkley notes a growing awareness that landscape architects are a valuable asset to a design team. As he says, "We are the ones who have a broad enough range of expertise to worry about the environmental concerns and other things to make the resulting projects user-friendly and earth-friendly."

Gardener and Groundskeeper

While landscape architects and related professionals are the ones who develop the designs, it is the gardeners and groundskeepers who implement the plans and maintain the work.

Landscape Services at Colonial Williamsburg

The landscape services department at Colonial Williamsburg employs about seventy full-time staff members who work year-round maintaining the gardens and landscape. The general positions within the department are entry-level groundskeeper jobs followed by a succession of gardener positions. Gardeners progress through three levels—A, B, and C; the highest gardener position is senior gardener. Gardeners are supervised by foremen, each of whom covers a particular area of the department. All supervisors manage three or four foremen and report directly to the departmental director.

The position of groundskeeper is basically an unskilled labor position. The groundskeeper supplies the gardening staff with the brawn to clean up and take care of things. Many groundskeepers have been trained for promotion to gardening positions. Gardener A is the entry-level position on the gardening ladder, and it requires only a minimum of skills. For instance, an employee in this position would have to know the difference between perennials and annuals, have some general knowledge of pruning and turf maintenance, and have some basic knowledge of chemicals, pesticides, herbicides, and fungicides, even though the job description does not include directly using them. To be promoted to a gardener B position, he or she would have to become a certified technician licensed for the use of pesticides by the requirements of the State of Virginia.

Gardener B works at a more professional level. A college degree is not required, but the gardener must be able to make appropriate calculations for the use of chemicals. Gardener B does all gardening chores and landscape maintenance, watering, pruning, fertilizing, planting, transplanting, bed working, and edging.

Gardener C must have a commercial pesticide license and is responsible for supervising groundskeepers. A gardener at this level is responsible for maintenance of a particular area of the landscape.

A senior gardener has similar but more extensive responsibilities as compared to a level-C gardener. The senior gardener makes sure that the staff gardeners have the material and equipment they need to do their work and fills in for the foreman if he or she is away, running the crews and keeping track of employees' time cards.

The foreman is in charge of a team that takes care of a large geographic area. A level-C gardener, for example, might be responsible for seven pieces of property, but a foreman might have fifteen or more. A college degree in botany or horticulture is preferred but not mandatory for a foreman position.

The department director manages the supervisors, who report directly to him or her. The director of landscape services reports to the director of landscape and facility services and also works closely with the landscape architect and garden historian.

A Topiary Trainer at Colonial Williamsburg

Wesley Greene is a member of the landscape services department at Colonial Williamsburg. He is a landscape supervisor who oversees the maintenance of the historic area gardens. He is also a licensed arborist in charge of the tree crew, and his special interest is topiary.

Greene started working in horticulture in 1978, in summer jobs during high school. He worked for the National Park Service, college campuses, and private industry. He has a bachelor's degree in botany from the University of Maine and has worked at Williamsburg since 1981.

Duties of a Landscape Supervisor

As landscape supervisor, Greene oversees twenty-six gardeners and tree surgeons. He describes his main function as "to train others, to give them the technical support, or sometimes a kick, whichever is required." He also does some designing and most of the topiary layout. Occasionally Greene does some of the actual topiary work himself because he enjoys it so much.

Lesson in Topiary

Greene describes the art of topiary, which comes from the Latin word *topiaries*, meaning ornamental gardener. It first arose during the Roman era. The first time the word *topiary* appeared referring to a plant training technique as opposed to the gardener was in an engraving of an arbor.

The art of topiary is the shaping of plants. Although most of us probably think of animals or geometric shapes as topiary, any shaped plant or trimmed hedge falls into the category.

There are two different kinds of topiary: those formed using wire structures and those formed without wire. An example of the wired type of topiary is what we might see at Disney theme parks; the nonwired type is exemplified by the horses and fox hunts of Ladew Gardens in Maryland.

"At Disney they use a wire form and let the plant grow around it, continuing to shape it as it grows," Greene explains. "We don't use wire forms at Williamsburg. We start with the plant and grow it into a shape."

Colonial Williamsburg has 178 acres of formal gardens, hedges, freestanding pieces, and topiary pieces that are incorporated into hedges. The designs include *estrade* topiary, which is a large round shape in a layer-cake design with a series of disks. There are also many plants shaped in squares, domes, and circles. Some flattop hedges have bubbles on top or diamonds shapes; some hedges sweep up at the corners.

Like everything else at Williamsburg, the topiary is based on eighteenth-century landscaping. Greene explains that by the middle of the 1700s, animal topiary was considered vulgar, which is why you won't see any animal shapes at Williamsburg.

Greene explains the basics of topiary: "To train topiary, you shear as you make the shape you want, but you have to keep a compact plant structure so it holds itself up in wind, rain, and snow, at the same time maintaining a straight central trunk. That's critical. If you lose the trunk you have to start over. Once we have overall shape, we lay it out. This is the Wesley Greene method; I use a little algebra here. I believe there's beauty in mathematics. There's a saying I made up: Formality by definition is wedded to geometry, and geometry by natural law is insufferable to approximation.

"That means you're exactly right or you don't show up!

"If you follow things mathematically, the eye picks up the repetition. Repetition sounds like a boring word, but it's the hallmark of good landscape design, repeating the forms, colors, and shapes throughout the garden design, or with topiary, within the individual piece."

Architectural Positions

Architectural historians, architectural conservators, curators of structures, restoration architects, and other preservationists all share a love of historic buildings and architecture. They might specialize in a particular period or style and be fascinated by Victorian gingerbread, strong red-brick or federal woodwork, and old frame farmhouses and barns. Most are generalists, however, with knowledge that crosses the centuries. These professionals are skilled researchers or artists and have strong organizational skills and an interest in the environment as well as history. In addition to working for private firms and individuals, many of these professionals offer their skills to history and living history museums utilizing historic buildings in their exhibits.

The activity of preservation includes several different categories, which are outlined here:

- **Adaptive reuse.** This process provides a new function for older structures that would otherwise be demolished. For example, a defunct mill is converted into an office building or a college.
- **Architectural conservation.** This process uses special techniques to halt further deterioration of building materials.
- **Restoration.** This process is often prefaced with "historical" or "architectural" and refers to meticulously returning a building to its former appearance at a particular period in history.
- **Rehabilitation or renovation.** This process alters or upgrades existing buildings and structures.

According to the National Association of Colleges and Employers, in 2002 the average starting salary for undergraduates in architecture working in nonprofit organizations was $33,471.

Architectural Conservator

Architectural conservators are not necessarily registered architects. They might have started out in the construction and contracting field and gained specialized technical experience in problems that occur with historic buildings. Some of these problems involve the historic building fabric, such as cracks in foundations and walls, water seepage, and how to clean the building. Architectural conservators understand how buildings were constructed during earlier periods and know what kinds of complications result from the natural course of time and different climatic and environmental conditions. They are familiar with building materials, roofs, windows, exterior cladding, and various construction types, such as wood frame or masonry-clad structures.

Restoration Architect

A restoration architect or an architect specializing in historic preservation has much of a general architect's experience. He or she understands how to plan spaces, how to organize construction materials, and how to put together construction documents.

The main difference between a general architect and a restoration architect is that the latter's work experience has primarily been focused on historic buildings. In addition, the restoration architect will have specialized knowledge and understanding of federal, state, and local regulations with regard to historic preservation, and he or she will be aware of the standards set by the particular style of architecture.

Architectural Historian

Architectural historians are historians with an interest in architecture. They are generally not registered architects. However, they often work with restoration architects, conducting specialized investigations and performing all the research necessary to get a restoration project going. They dig up a building's history—researching when it was constructed, its original purpose, how long it was vacant, and whether any changes had been made. Then they put together a historic structures report for the architect who wants to make his or her restoration work as accurate as possible.

In addition to museum settings, architectural historians can work in academic settings, for private architectural firms, and for government agencies concerned with historic preservation.

The minimum requirement for an architectural historian is an undergraduate degree in history or architectural history, although most positions require a graduate degree.

Historic Interiors Designer

To achieve complete authenticity, the interior of a historic building must be given as much attention as the exterior, especially if the building will be used as a museum open to the public.

Historic interiors designers can be architects or specially trained professionals. They must be experienced in the investigation, documentation, research, and analysis of the lighting, furnishings, finishes, and decorative arts of building interiors. Historic interiors specialists generally work as part of a team with the restoration architect and conservator.

6

NATURAL HISTORY MUSEUMS

THE MISSION OF a natural history museum is to preserve, research, interpret, and exhibit the evidence of natural and cultural science of specific eras or regions throughout the world.

Job Titles in Natural History Museums

The job titles you will find in natural history museums are similar to those found in other museums. The difference, of course, is in the collections with which the various professionals work and their educational background and training. For example, art museum conservators work with paintings; natural history museum conservators work with a variety of objects. A curator for an art museum will have studied fine arts; an art history curator for a natural history museum will have studied any one or more of the sciences relevant to the museum.

Throughout this chapter we will look at the different career paths in natural history museums.

Director

The director is responsible for the overall running of the museum. In conjunction the board of directors, the director helps to determine and implement the mission of the museum.

The Carnegie Museum of Natural History

The Carnegie Museum of Natural History in Pittsburgh, Pennsylvania, is the fifth-largest natural history museum in the United States, with a collection of more than seventeen million specimens and artifacts. It is also one of the nation's largest private research museums that is not associated with a university. The museum has three major components: a large education program, including outreach, which reaches three hundred thousand people a year outside the museum facility; an exhibit component; and research.

Collections are worldwide in distribution and focus on traditional natural history areas including botany, zoology, geology, paleontology, minerals, gems, and anthropology.

Director of the Carnegie Museum of Natural History

Dr. James King served as director of the Carnegie Museum of Natural History from 1987 until 2001. He attended Alma College, a small liberal arts college in Alma, Michigan, and graduated with a B.A. in biology. Although his career plans were uncertain, he became very interested in the study of pollen grains. He went on to the University of New Mexico and earned his master's and then got his doctorate in geology at the University of Arizona in Tucson.

King taught at Arizona for a while and then received a large National Science Foundation Grant with a colleague to do archaeological work on extinct animals. He worked at a museum in Illinois, moving up through the ranks from assistant curator to full curator to chief scientist and then to assistant director for science before coming to the Carnegie. Here King talks about the job and why he believes that natural history museums are so important to society.

"The main thing that attracts me to natural history museum work," King explains, "is that I am deeply concerned about the quality of science education in this country. It's going to affect the future of this country. I think we all see the social problems we have in the world today and in the United States. Education has always been a way to get out of poverty, a way to get ahead.

"Museums fit a unique role in that we are a major part of the informal science education network. One of the things that excites me and intrigues me about our institution is the contribution we can make to that network."

Toward this goal of providing education, King points to the "user-friendly" aspect of natural history museums. He describes the visible joy of the hundreds of thousands of young students who visit the museum every year. Children enjoy the museum because they are able to gain some real meaning from the information they are taking in. For example, while children marvel at the massive prehistoric creatures in the hall of dinosaurs, educators can discuss a number of scientific topics such as the age of the earth, extinction, and so on.

As a researcher, King also believes that natural history museums provide the ideal setting to conduct research. As he says, "Museums, as far as I'm concerned, are a better location to do this than a university. We have the collections, and second, you're not saddled with teaching duties. A beginning professor always has courses to teach. Here, a beginning curator has a lot more time to work on his or her research."

Duties of the Director

As museum director, King was responsible for all aspects of the institution. He met four times each year with the board to review directions and policies that he was ultimately responsible for implementing. King also worked closely with his management committee, which included the head of the exhibit department, head of the education department, assistant director for sciences, and assistant director for administration.

King's daily activities were similar to those of any director of a large institution. On the administrative side, for example, he had to make sure that necessary repairs were made to the heating system as well as handle financial matters or personnel issues. As he says, the director is "the mediator, the court of last resort."

About 25 percent of King's time was spent on fund-raising. He spent most of his time, however, leading and guiding the staff and board of directors, making decisions that would affect the future of the museum. Diplomacy is a big factor in a director's daily interactions, a fact that King illustrates by describing "the care and feeding of the board of directors." King explains that board members often contacted him with ideas for exhibits or improvements, and while some ideas were good, others required him to say no.

For example, King tells of a board member who suggested that the museum put live butterflies in the exhibit hall. Although the public would have welcomed the idea, King had to point out that butterflies require very high humidity and warm temperatures, which are not possible in the museum's old marble galleries.

The museum also offers cultural programs to members. One such program includes travel with a board member, curator, or the director to a special destination. King traveled with a group to Kenya for big-game viewing and to Antarctica for whale-watching and viewing penguins. Another whale-watching trip was to Cape Cod. The trips focus on areas with interesting history, geology, and sightseeing possibilities.

"The trips are fun, but they are also a lot of work," King says. "You have to look after people—lugging suitcases in Africa for a woman who was having back trouble, trying to straighten out ticket messes in Nairobi. In Antarctica I had to arrange to leave a woman at a Chilean Navy base because she'd fallen on the ship and broken an arm."

No director can be truly successful without a support staff, and King is quick to praise the people who worked for him. He proudly said, "My favorite part of my job is watching some of the world's greatest staff, that's ours, just do good things. They're expected to raise grant funds to support their research, expected to publish, to have a national—even international—reputation. When a curator gets a major paper published in a journal or gets a new grant on something, that's probably the best part of my job.

"It also pleases me no end to get letters from people saying things like, 'My son's third-grade class was in your museum and one of your educators just did a sterling job.' That really makes me feel good. I can talk about us being a world-famous research museum with millions of items in our collections, but our greatest asset is really our staff."

Advice from James King

King points out that a degree in museum studies is not a requirement for working in this field. He recommends a good education that will provide a solid foundation in your chosen area, whether it is science, teaching, or an artistic field.

In King's experience, the majority of people hired at the museum have traditional academic backgrounds and are not necessarily "museum study people." Most have at least a bachelor's degree in a field related to natural science, such as anthropology or geology. Some employees take short courses in museum techniques.

King suggests talking with people who work in natural history museums. He says, "I probably talk to half a dozen people a month here who want to know about careers in museums. I'll talk to them for a while, and then if they're interested in science, I may have them spend an hour or two talking to a curator. Or they may go up and spend time in our education program, just watching."

Volunteering is also an important step in starting a career in a natural history museum. In King's experience, it is a valuable way to learn what the work involves and whether it is right for you.

Conservator

Most conservators in natural history museums work in collaboration with other professionals on the staff. Very often the conservator and curator consult to discuss how to handle a damaged piece. Conservators also deal with the exhibits department. The conservator tells the exhibit designers how they can build a mount for an object so that the object is supported. They provide much of the information that is displayed on labels, and arrange for proper lighting levels so the colors do not fade.

Conservators also work closely with exhibit designers and curators when they are planning a new show or transporting objects. How an object is supported or wrapped so it can go to another museum without damage is another task that often falls into the conservator's realm.

And though working with visiting scholars often is part of a collection manager's job, conservators often instruct students about the correct way to handle an object.

A Conservator at the Carnegie Museum of Natural History

An objects conservator for a natural history museum will probably see a wider range of items than a conservator at an art museum. Joan Gardner, chief conservator at the Carnegie Museum of Natural History, works with a variety of anthropological objects including skins, hides, furs, Indian robes, wooden dolls, and feathered headdresses.

Many of these garments and items were not meant to last longer than a few years, but some of them have now lasted several hundred. A conservator's efforts show long-lasting results.

Duties of the Conservator

The main objective of Gardner's work as conservator is to preserve the integrity of an object in its present state. Unlike restoration, conservation does not strive to return an item to its original condition. Rather, conservators strive to slow further deterioration. Gardner says, "We wouldn't take a sword that's ancient and make it shiny and look as if it were fabricated the day before yesterday. That's not our purpose."

If a degree of repair work is necessary, conservators try to use only materials that are compatible with the original item and its time in history. They are careful not to use anything that is anachronistic or that could damage the object in any way.

Gardner describes one project that involves working with a bentwood box from the northwest coast Haida Indians. When she receives a new object, Gardner researches the materials it was made from, how it was made, and the colorants used. She takes samples and sends them off for analysis to try to determine what the origin of the dye or paint was.

This particular box was badly abraded and broken in many places; in addition, steel nails had been hammered into it. Gardner's first step is to document exactly what the box looks like when she first sees it, noting where the breaks are and where modern materials have been used on it. She documents the colors, the design, and the technique that was used to make the object.

The conservators are meticulous in their documentation, noting the exact size and location of each abrasion. They photograph the item before working on it, during the working process, and after they have finished. Gardner describes this part of the process by saying, "What we're really trying to do is document what an object is made of, what we used on it, and why we did it, so there's a record for history. We're record keepers as well as people who intervene."

Following this initial documentation, Gardner will remove any modern materials from the box and will apply adhesives that are reversible. The logic behind this step is to ensure that if a better substance is devised in the future, the adhesive can be removed and replaced with the new material.

In the case of the damaged bentwood box, Gardner says that she would not try to "fix" the abrasions in the object. She would attempt to obscure some of the worst ones so that the box looks to be in better condition. While she can tone down the abrasions, she would nevertheless document every step so that the intent of the original item is not lost in the process. As she says, "You don't want to obscure the original artist's work at all."

Gardner has also worked with elaborate headdresses from several Native American tribes. The headdresses are often quite large and made with dyed horse hair, eagle feathers, and painted wood.

She has worked with Kachina dolls produced by the Hopi tribes of the Southwest. The dolls, which represent different spirits, were used to appeal to the gods for rain or other needs and as a training tool for children in the household. The dolls are usually made of wood and have adornments such as bows and arrows and feathered headdresses. Most of them are also painted and wear complex outfits. The amount of documentation that such objects require is truly daunting.

Working at the Carnegie Museum of Natural History presents an interesting problem for conservators. Pittsburgh has long been an industrial city, and soot and pollution particles come right through the building and settle on the objects that are not enclosed. In the museum's early years, most objects were displayed on open shelves, and many have accumulated a great deal of soot and dirt that obscure their colors and detail. One of the conservators' biggest and most challenging jobs is to try to remove the soot without damaging or diluting the objects' pigments.

It is this direct contact with the items in the collections that Gardner likes best. She says, "For me, working with the object is the best part of my job, dealing with the colors and the textures and the research to see what's happened to it in the past.

"It's such a constant challenge, and as much as I love it, sometimes I get weary. It's a big job, overwhelming, and sometimes you can't really put it to bed at night. I do a lot of reading in the evenings to find out, for example, what the latest feather-cleaning technique is. I go through a lot of journals to find an article that's pertinent. That for me is the only downside. I love what I do."

Gardner worked as a science and math teacher and as a social worker before deciding to return to school and change careers. A long-standing fascination with anthropology and archaeology helped her to decide which direction to take.

"You can't get into this profession without being fascinated with the objects that people produce in various cultures around the world, what these objects mean, and why they're done the way they are," Gardner says. "They're often so beautiful, but you just don't know, until you get into anthropology, what it all means. Sometimes you don't even know then."

For her master's degree, Gardner was enrolled in a special studies program with an emphasis in conservation. The program was divided between anthropology and art history, with an emphasis on chemistry. During her studies, she was part of a joint program with George Washington University and the Smithsonian Institution. When Gardner encountered the Smithsonian's program in museum studies with a conservation component, she knew that this was what she wanted to study.

Gardner served her internship at the Smithsonian during the entire three years of her graduate studies. She describes the experience as similar to working a full-time job, fitting classes between her hours at the Smithsonian. Gardner received her master's degree in 1976 and immediately began working at the Carnegie Museum.

Advice from Joan Gardner

Gardner has a specific recommendation for anyone interested in pursuing this field. "Before you go for your master's," she says, "you have to demonstrate a good knowledge of chemistry, you have to be good with your hands, and you have to be really bright. Almost every student has some talent, in painting, pottery, working with metals. Most people have a portfolio before they go on for their master's."

Studying for a master's degree will teach you theory as well as provide practical experience. Once you have received your degree, you can choose an area of specialization. Gardner suggests that if you know while in school which particular area you are interested in pursuing, it is a good idea to find a museum where you can serve an internship in that area.

As an example, Gardner cites an assistant conservator at the Carnegie Museum who spent his studies working on many kinds of objects, handling different materials, and conducting analysis and research projects. When he realized that he wanted to work with Native American material, he secured an internship at Arizona State Museum, which specializes in anthropological and archaeological objects. The experience he gained during the internship, combined with his educational program, led him to a job in conservation at the Carnegie.

Gardner offers some advice for aspiring conservators: "It's a wonderful profession, but you have to have an awful lot of skill. Not only must you master the information, but you have to be able to deal with things that require an awful lot of patience. My master's work involved unfolding and stabilizing some fabrics that were in a mound, buried in A.D. 1200. They were so dry, you would touch them and they'd shatter in your hands. Frankly, it's not something that most people have the patience for."

Job Outlook for Conservators

By the time you graduate with your master's, you will be a skilled conservator. Unfortunately, walking into a job in a natural history museum is not a given. Not every natural history museum employs a conservator. Some museums contract work out to private conservators because the cost of keeping a full-time conservator on staff can be prohibitive. Even museums that do employ a conservator occasionally use private contractors for large projects, such as setting up a new exhibit hall.

Obviously the larger the museum the more likely it is to employ one or more full-time conservators. Starting a private conservation practice can be costly, but the financial rewards can be high once your reputation is established.

Taxidermy

The art of preparing, preserving, and mounting the skin, hair, feathers, or scales of animals in a lifelike position for study or display is called *taxidermy*. The word is derived from the Greek *taxis*, "to arrange," and *derma*, "skin."

Techniques vary with the kind of animal, but in all cases the skin is removed, cleaned, and chemically treated with a preservative. It is then placed on a prepared model made of material that will withstand insects and changes in humidity and temperature. The model is sculptured to replicate the exact size and shape of the animal and can be placed in whatever pose is desired.

Taxidermy is a highly specialized art. Taxidermists must have thorough knowledge of anatomy, natural history, drawing, sculpture, mechanics, dyeing, and leather tanning.

Job prospects for taxidermists with natural history museums are very slim. According to Dr. King of the Carnegie Museum of Natural History, "We don't do major taxidermy any more; no major museum does. There's really no need any more for mounting big animals. We all have them already."

As an example, the American Museum of Natural History in New York at one time had nine full-time taxidermists on its staff. Now it has none. Carnegie had a full taxidermy department until the 1960s. Now it employs a full-time sculptor, who also does some taxidermy work when needed.

There is, however, a demand for repair work and occasionally some taxidermy of small birds and animals. In addition, taxidermists can find work outside of natural history museums, for example, in mounting trophies for hunters and fishermen.

Educator

Educators usually possess a teaching certificate or have gained teaching experience before joining a museum staff. They arrange public programs explaining the exhibits, conduct classes, and often do outreach work with local schools and other community organizations. Tour guides, or docents, as they are often called, usually fall under the realm of the education department.

Editor and Writer

Most museums produce in-house publications—brochures, pamphlets, newsletters, catalogs, books, and other promotional material. Editors and writers usually have a college degree and strong editorial skills.

Exhibit Personnel

Exhibit personnel include artisans and designers, who plan the exhibits; cabinetmakers, who build the wood cases for the exhibits; sculptors, who make miniatures and models for the exhibits; taxidermists, who mount the skins and hides of animals in lifelike positions for study and display; silk screeners, who do all the label work; artists and scientific illustrators, who provide sketches and detailed drawings of the different objects; and CAD systems professionals, who work with computer-aided designs to translate the sketches and drawings of proposed designs and exhibits into finished blueprints. Exhibit personnel usually have strong art backgrounds.

Collections Personnel

The professionals who track and maintain the collections include curators, researchers, and conservators, all of whom usually have Ph.D. degrees. Assistant curators or collections managers assist these professionals in their work. Assistants generally possess either a bachelor's or a master's degree.

Public Programs and Services Personnel

Almost all museums provide some sort of educational programming for the public. Educators and program developers design classes, workshops, lectures, and tours and often offer outreach programs to the schools or local community in which they are located.

Volunteer Coordinator and Interns

Most museums rely heavily on volunteer staff in addition to their paid employees. The volunteer coordinator usually works with these volunteers (see Chapter 7). Students who participate in internship programs are usually supervised by the curator or other professional to whom they are assigned.

Archaeologist

Many natural history museums have full-time archaeologists on staff or work with archaeologists who also have appointments at universities. During the summer months, college students, and even sometimes high school students, are brought on board to help out with summer field programs.

The Profession of Archaeology

Archaeology is a subdivision of the field of anthropology. Archaeologists study the artifacts of past cultures in order to learn about their history, customs, and living habits. They survey and excavate archaeological sites and record and catalog their finds. By careful analysis, archaeologists reconstruct earlier cultures and determine their influence on the present.

Archaeological sites are the physical remains of past civilizations. They can include building debris and the items found inside—in addition to trash. Usually these sites have been buried by other, later human activity or by natural processes.

Excavation of these sites is a painstaking process conducted by professionals using modern techniques. Because these sites are so fragile, the very nature of excavating destroys some information. With this in mind, archaeologists are careful to dig only as much as they need to answer important questions. Frequently, archaeologists concentrate their work on sites slated to be destroyed, such as for highway or new building construction.

Archaeologists conducting fieldwork often work with several other professionals in a team effort. They are assisted by curators, conservators, geologists, ethnologists, educators, anthropologists, ecologists, and aerial photographers.

In the field, archaeologists use a variety of tools during an excavation. These include picks, shovels, trowels, wheelbarrows, sifting boxes, pressure sprayers, and brushes. Archaeologists also make drawings and sketches on-site as well as take notes and photographs.

Educational Preparation

To qualify as a professional archaeologist, graduate study leading to a master's degree is necessary. A doctoral degree is often preferable. Most graduate programs in archaeology are found in anthropology departments. There are about thirty or so universities maintaining schools of archaeology; these can be found listed in *Peterson's Guide to Graduate and Professional Programs*. (Visit www.petersons.com for information.) To gain the necessary background on the under-graduate level, a study of anthropology, history, art, geology, or a related field should be pursued. At the graduate level, students fol-lowing a course in archaeology would also have to include cultural and physical anthropology as well as linguistics in their curriculum.

7

SCIENCE MUSEUMS AND DISCOVERY CENTERS

IN THE PAST, traditional science museums tended to focus on the historical implications of their collections, and the staff members were likely to be scholars who conducted research and concerned themselves with the preservation and display of objects.

Today, the main focus of many museums of science, discovery, and technology has switched to teaching. Collections and artifacts, while still important, take a back seat to active, participatory exhibits designed to help visitors become better acquainted with scientific and technological principles. Staff members in science and technology centers are more likely to be scientists with an interest in teaching, rather than being straight researchers.

But many traditional museums have begun to successfully combine the two approaches, incorporating hands-on and participatory programs in their exhibits. Some have special discovery rooms; others integrate these elements into existing or new exhibits.

Among those that mix the two approaches, with an emphasis on the teaching aspects, are the Museum of Science and Industry in Chicago and the Museum of Science in Boston, both profiled in this chapter.

The number of science centers in which almost exclusive attention is paid to teaching is rapidly increasing. In many cases, these centers have been developed to augment school curricula or to fill a vacuum where school courses have not been available. All strive to show science as a fascinating subject, to entertain while educating, and to reach a wider audience. The Museum of Discovery and Science in Fort Lauderdale, also profiled in this chapter, is just one example.

Job Titles in Science Museums and Discovery Centers

The hallmark of discovery and science centers is that almost all exhibits are hands-on, participatory experiences that educate visitors in an exciting and fun-filled way. Exhibits might include activities that allow you to operate a waterwheel, ride a tractor, or encase yourself in a bubble.

With all the activity that occurs in a discovery center, it's not surprising that a large staff is required to maintain the exhibits and assist patrons. Here is a sample of some of the career areas you might encounter in this setting:

Collections manager
Community outreach manager
Curator
Directors of exhibits, programs, special projects, and
   natural science

Educator
Exhibit builder/fabricator
Graphic designer
President/CEO
Teacher/training coordinator
Technician
Vice president of development
Vice president of finance/chief financial officer
Vice president of marketing and quality services
Vice president of programs and exhibits
Vice president of research and business development
Youth programs manager

As we have seen in the previous chapters, many museum careers are found in just about every type of museum, but some are specific to the mission of the particular establishment. In this chapter we will hear from two professionals whose job titles are shaped by working in a science museum or discovery center.

Collections Manager at the Museum of Science and Industry

Not all museums employ a traditional curatorial system. In a science museum, for example, the standard system is often replaced by a more open system in which the collections department assumes the functions of curator. Some professionals believe that this method allows for a more balanced approach to exhibits because curators aren't trying to push for exhibits in their own specific areas.

The Chicago Museum of Science and Industry is one of the largest in the country, covering fourteen and a half acres and housing a collection of approximately eighty thousand objects.

The museum's collections manager, Mike Sarna, explains that the collection is actually small, since this is a hands-on museum. He cites the museum's exhibit on AIDS to illustrate his point. Although the exhibit contains very few artifacts, it does have "Star Wars–type interactives" that teach children about the disease and its prevention. In Sarna's view, the same exhibit at a historical society museum would most likely include a range of artifacts detailing the history of the disease. The Museum of Science and Industry aims to demonstrate physical properties.

Another interactive exhibit is a 727 aircraft that is actually inside the museum building. The exhibit takes the plane through a simulated flight from San Francisco to Chicago. It is on a raised balcony, so that viewers looking up from below can see the flaps and landing gear working throughout the multimedia program. Inside the plane is an "uncommon classroom," where visitors learn about the flight.

In addition to his role as collections manager at the Museum of Science and Industry, Sarna is also the registrar and director of collections, as well as director of one of the eight thematic zones into which the museum is divided. He came to the museum in 1993 with a bachelor's degree in history and museum studies from the University of Iowa in Iowa City (1987) and a master's degree in historical administration (museum studies) from Eastern Illinois University in Charleston, Illinois (1991). He also brought with him a wealth of experience from other museums such as the DuSable Museum of African-American History in Chicago; the Aurora Historical Museum (Illinois); the Lisle Depot Museum (Illinois); and the Chicago Historical Society.

Sarna's initial college major was pharmacy, but he was not very happy with that choice. He loved history but did not want to teach in a traditional classroom setting. In considering what other options he could have as a history major, Sarna took a class in museum studies and was hooked right away. He says, "I'm a teacher now with this job, in a different sort of way. I'm a social historian, not a scientist, although I've picked up a lot of science along the way. But our collection is more a history of science."

Duties of a Collection Manager

The main responsibility of a collections manager is the proper storage and mounting of the artifacts. The job also includes conservation, since the manager must care for and oversee the collection. The Museum of Science and Industry employs a conservation technician who takes necessary measures to clean or repair an item that is going on exhibit.

The collections manager is also responsible for keeping track of where things are in the museum with inventories. Sarna makes up object worksheets, which list the dimensions, condition, physical properties, and historical research of every object in the collection. He is also responsible for putting together catalogs.

As manager, Sarna is responsible for staffing and any personnel issues that arise. He supervises thirty staff members in the various departments, including a collections assistant who works with the artifacts and conducts research when anyone calls to ask if the museum has a particular item.

Sarna talks about one of the best aspects of his job. "There's a lot of variety to the position," he says. "You get into one subject, you work on an exhibit or you catalog a collection or you do this or that, then you move on to another subject and learn about that. For someone with eclectic interests, this is a great job. In some museum jobs you might be pigeonholed. You sit down at your desk and work on one specific collection. I manage staff members who work on a lot of different exhibits.

"It's very exciting work, dealing with one-of-a-kind artifacts on the culture of America. It's a privilege to work in a museum.

"We have tons of projects. We're a very busy department because we're usually involved with anything that happens in this museum. There's usually always an artifact involved in some way. And we also do a very good job. People who do good jobs usually get more work to do."

Advice from Mike Sarna

Sarna is an advocate of an advanced degree as a way to succeed in museum work. He advises getting a master's degree and finding the right internship. Although many smaller museums offer paid internships, many larger museums of note might not. In Sarna's opinion, it is beneficial to take an unpaid internship at a larger institution to gain the most experience.

Sarna says, "If you're serious and the Smithsonian should offer you an unpaid internship for three months, take it."

Salaries at Science Museums

Expect to receive low pay when you start, Sarna warns. "Museums are not for profit. Our salaries here are very competitive, but it's one of the top museums. Generally, museum salaries are low. Once you get into management, you're going to get more."

Collections assistants and archivists might start in the low thirties, an assistant registrar in the high thirties, and management positions in the forties or fifties, depending on experience and location of the facility.

Director of Special Projects at the Museum of Discovery and Science in Fort Lauderdale

The Museum of Discovery and Science in Fort Lauderdale, Florida, opened in 1977 as a small museum with the goal of providing science education for children. The focus was primarily the elementary schoolchild. Now the Museum of Science and Discovery is a place for all ages. In November of 1992, the museum opened in a new facility with a new focus. "We had to broaden our audience base," exaplains its director of special projects, "and we didn't want to be perceived as just a children's museum. Now we see all different ages; the family is still our predominant audience, and schools bring their kids in."

The museum has eighty-five thousand square feet of space. About thirty-five thousand feet are used for exhibits, and the rest is for behind-the-scenes activities.

There is an IMAX theater that is five stories high and has twenty-two speakers. There are seven exhibit areas on two levels: the KidScience area; a health area; a Florida environment area called Florida Ecoscapes, which is the museum's signature exhibit; a sound exhibit; a space exhibit; a technology exhibit; and a traveling exhibit hall, which has featured such exhibits as "Backyard Monsters" and "Tuskegee Airmen."

Joyce Williams is the director of special projects at the Museum of Discovery and Science in Fort Lauderdale. She earned her B.S. degree in science education with a minor in adolescent psychology from Cornell University in Ithaca, New York, and her M.S. degree in adult education/human resource development at Florida International University in Miami.

Williams taught science at the middle and high school levels in Florida. In 1986 the director of education at the Museum of Discovery and Science offered her a summer job; by the end of the summer, the administration had created a full-time position as a science education specialist for Williams.

After two years Williams was promoted to an associate director of education. In 1993 she was offered a position as a director of program and special projects. As the department has grown, the position split into two: one for a director of programs and the other for Williams's current position as the director of special projects.

Duties of a Director of Special Projects

As director, Williams's primary concern is audience development, which means making sure that the museum reaches underrepresented populations such as preschoolers, senior citizens, or those in diverse ethnic groups. Williams's responsibilities involve establishing collaborative relationships with the community. She looks for partners either in industry or in other educational institutions for the museum's programs and exhibits, such as meeting with the Broward Center for the Performing Arts to set up a performing arts collaborative.

Williams sees collaboration as the wave of the future for science museums and discovery centers. Given the fact that many institutions have a vast amount of information to impart but limited resources with which to do it, collaborative efforts make sense as the best way to reach the public. This eliminates repetition and allows for more sophisticated exhibits. Williams is fortunate to be a long-standing member of the community, so she has many contacts she can turn to when trying to set up a program.

As an example of this aspect of her work, Williams says that the local library and Head Start program want to collaborate with the museum. In this case, she will inquire about what they have in mind and will work to determine whether there is a point of common ground among the three institutions. Once a common thread is established, Williams will work with representatives from the other two organizations to put together the best possible program.

Sometimes a potential partner wants to reach the same target audience or use the same methodology that the museum employs. "As an example," Williams says, "Motorola has a big industry, but maybe they don't have access to the general public. We might be doing a technology project. So we could go to them for their expertise because we could never afford the state-of-the-art technology that comes out every month. They might supply the technology and the content expertise, and we are the experts at displaying things, and we also know what the general public is looking for."

Williams believes that participatory museums can make a difference in educating children, and even adults, by illustrating the real application of science. "Science is fascinating," Williams says, "but most people don't have that impression. I think that museums have a unique opportunity to bring science to life and to show that it's not something to be afraid of and that it's fun. It's also very creative, and we can do it in an entertaining way. We can also make a difference in the classroom, training teachers how to use a different approach to teaching science.

"We hope that people will become more comfortable with science and perhaps even go into science as a career. It's a very friendly field. And I like that we perform an important function, involving people in science. You want to do something that's going to have an impact."

Advice from Joyce Williams

Williams recommends volunteering as a way to decide whether working in a museum is right for you. This will allow you to learn the museum's mission and goals and to prepare yourself to pursue those same goals.

If you are interested in working in a museum's education department, Williams believes that experience as a teacher is very helpful. She says many of her colleagues have backgrounds in teaching.

Williams's experience allows her to make an interesting observation about her field. "I don't think people go to museums to be educated; they go to be entertained," she says. "A person who wants to go into this field can't be an authoritarian teacher. And a person would need either a broad-based basic science background or a specialization in an area of science. And the arts are important, a theater background would help, as well as teaching skills and a love for people. You should have the substance, the entertaining delivery that makes it palatable, and the educational background to know what different ages are capable of learning and how people learn."

Finding a Job in a Science Center

The Association of Science-Technology Centers (ASTC) maintains a job bank that lists positions available at science centers throughout the United States. To find out about the job bank and to also receive a list of hands-on science centers near you, contact:

ASTC
1025 Vermont Avenue NW, Suite 500
Washington, DC 20005-6310
astc.org

Volunteer Coordinator at the Museum of Science, Boston

As mentioned throughout this book, most museums rely heavily on volunteers to run their many programs. In addition, volunteering is often a way to learn of permanent positions and to get your foot in the door for that plum job you've been hoping to land.

Mary Alice Dwyer came to the Museum of Science in 1986 with a college degree in English and a lifetime of experience as a volunteer. Through a friend, she found out that the museum was looking for a part-time coordinator. She had two interviews and was hired for the job. After working part-time for only three days, she was hired on a full-time basis.

Dwyer interviews new volunteers and tries to match each applicant with the needs of the various departments to best utilize the volunteers' skills. She keeps track of the volunteers' hours and maintains a recognition program that annually acknowledges volunteer work based on the number of hours they have served.

When new volunteers begin their tours, Dwyer provides orientation and conducts a "get-acquainted-with-the-museum" program. The volunteers are given a handbook of volunteer guidelines and are taken around the museum so that they can become familiar with emergency procedures. In an effort to keep things light, Dwyer sends the volunteers on a scavenger hunt as a way of helping them learn their way around the museum. This ensures that when visitors ask them directions about the museum, they will be able to answer correctly.

The volunteer coordinator's office is an extemely busy place, with departments calling to request help with special projects and potential volunteers calling for information about positions. Dwyer meets with department heads and recruits volunteers for special events. She also assists with fund-raising during the museum's annual Fourth of July event, which alone requires approximately one hundred volunteers.

Since the museum is open evenings and weekends, Dwyer has to be flexible about her working hours. She occasionally takes work home from the office. She stresses the importance of organizational skills in this job and the need to be friendly and patient, since she deals with many different types of people.

Of course, a successful volunteer coordinator needs volunteers to work with, and Dwyer is quick to praise those at the Museum of Science. She says, "We have marvelous volunteers. Obviously, with our location we get many retired people from MIT, Harvard, and the rest of the academic scene. They're quality people. We have a lot of junior volunteers, too, who are very enthusiastic, and it's delightful to see them come up through the ranks and then go on to become staff in summer jobs. We also have our young professionals with varied backgrounds. It's a real potpourri.

"Our volunteers serve every department in the museum and gave sixty-seven thousand hours last year. We have six hundred volunteers; they're the equivalent of thirty-six paid employees."

To sum up her experience, Dwyer says, "I like working with all the different people and sending the right person to the right job. When you make a good match, it benefits the volunteer and also benefits the museum. And you want to make sure the volunteers are happy where they've been placed.

"There's not one negative to it. There's always a challenge, and you're always busy so you're never bored. It's a rewarding job. It's been a wonderful experience."

Volunteer Opportunities at the Museum of Science, Boston

Although each museum probably runs its volunteer program differently, many of the components will be the same. As an example, here is a close-up look at the volunteer program at the Museum of Science in Boston.

The Museum of Science features many volunteer opportunities in a variety of programs. Most volunteer positions ask for three to four hours a week on a regular basis (for at least six months), weekdays or weekends depending on the specific job. The museum provides excellent benefits for volunteers, including free parking and admission, discounts in restaurants and shops, training, and more.

Here is a sample of some of the departments in which a volunteer could be placed:

- **Live animal center.** This is where exotic animals used in education demonstrations are housed. Volunteers assist with cleaning cages and handling and taking care of these animals.
- **Discovery center.** This area contains many hands-on materials such as rocks, bones, stethoscopes, and more. Volunteers should love small children and families and enjoy informally teaching science through doing.
- **Computer discovery.** Space volunteers do not need to be computer whizzes, but they should be interested in computers and want to learn.

- **Life sciences.** Volunteers in this area will demonstrate the dissection of a sheep's heart or the reproductive system of a flower, for example. Life science interpreters should also enjoy human biology and working with other volunteers and staff.
- **Information desk.** These volunteers are stationed in the lobby of the museum. They are front-line resources for visitors, answering questions on entrance fees, exhibits, upcoming events, and location of museum facilities, among others.
- **Curatorial department.** These volunteers work as part of two-person teams to video artifacts from the museum's collection. Needed are individuals who are highly motivated and like to work with computers and video equipment. Training is provided.

Other areas in which the Museum of Science utilizes the services of volunteers are in the museum shop, in the library, in membership sales, as birthday party volunteers, for office work, and for physical science interpretation. The museum also has a junior volunteer program for fourteen- to eighteen-year-olds.

By contacting the museum and asking for the volunteer department (see Appendix C for addresses of the institutions profiled here), you will receive a volunteer information packet with full job descriptions and application forms.

By definition, volunteers are unpaid workers. However, there is usually one paid position in a museum involving volunteering, and that is the volunteer coordinator, the person who oversees the volunteer program.

Salaries for Volunteer Coordinators

As with any nonprofit career, salaries for volunteer coordinators aren't particularly high. Even in a big city you could expect to earn only in the low to midtwenties. However, the position of volunteer coordinator can be used as a stepping-stone to other administrative positions. The farther up the administrative ladder you go, the higher the salaries.

8

PLANETARIUMS

MOST OF US have visited a planetarium at one time or another and can recall the thrill of sitting in a darkened dome and watching the night sky spread above and around us. With an impressive voice explaining the spectacle, we witnessed solar and lunar eclipses, the solar corona, comets, auroras, the configuration of the Milky Way, and other astronomical phenomena.

While many of us were content to view the experience as a form of educational entertainment, a small few, perhaps those of you reading this book, wondered how all the special effects were achieved and how you might make the world of planetariums a part of your future career.

Job Titles in Planetariums

As you read this chapter and consider the magnitude of the planetarium shows that are profiled, it will become clear that it takes many people with varied skills to put together something so complex and so intricately detailed. Here is a summary of some of the jobs involved.

Producer

The producer brings together all the elements of a show. Media experience is important, as well as the ability to manage groups and to make sound judgments and decisions.

Technician

Technicians construct, maintain, and install stationary exhibits and may make sound tracks or special-effects devices. A bachelor's degree or degree from a technical or trade school, and related experience, are usually required for this position.

Artist

Artists create images for use in planetarium shows. Computer graphics, airbrushing, and other media are used in many instances.

Astronomer

Astronomers translate research into information accessible to the general public. Planetariums that are affiliated with universities or have an observatory employ staff astronomers who teach and conduct research. A doctorate is usually required; a master's degree is acceptable in some cases.

Educational Programmer/Coordinator

The educational programmer/coordinator develops ideas for shows and conducts the necessary research materials for producing them.

A background in astronomy is a plus, and a master's degree is required for most jobs in this area.

Scriptwriter

Scriptwriters use information and research to write the narrative portions of shows. A scriptwriter might be on staff at a planetarium or could work as a freelancer.

Presenter

Presenters handle the live portions of shows and interact with the audience, which often consists of schoolchildren. Good communication skills are a plus.

The Hayden Sphere

In February 2000, after extensive renovation, New York's Hayden Planetarium reopened as the Hayden Sphere. The largest and most powerful virtual-reality simulator in the world, the Hayden Sphere is part of the Rose Center for Earth and Space at the American Museum of Natural History (part of the Smithsonian Institution).

The heart of the planetarium is the Space Theater, where "Passport to the Universe," a three-dimensional space ride, is presented. A one-of-a-kind projector and digital system are used to fly audiences through the galaxy and beyond. Simulated flight made possible by the largest data-based model of the universe ever projected lets the viewer virtually travel to the surface of any object in the solar system.

The Hayden Sphere's show is based on actual astronomical data and computer models of our galaxy obtained from the National

Aeronautics and Space Administration (NASA), including the Hubble Space Telescope. Other sources include a statistical database of more than three billion stars developed by the museum. For sections of the galaxy for which there are no available data, the museum constructed statistical models that were translated into high-definition computer simulations of the galaxy.

The projector used in the Hayden Sphere is fully controlled by computer and can project more than nine thousand stars onto the dome, along with the sun and planets. Thirty times each second, the supercomputer calculates the real location and appearance of every star and nebula that is about to be seen by the audience. Fiber optics generates a starry sky that includes objects normally viewable only through binoculars.

Scientists, imagery analysts, programmers, graphic designers, and educators are building a visual database of the two hundred thousand observed stars, pulsars, and nebulae that have been charted in astronomical catalogs. The computer system can generate statistically correct stars to represent the two hundred million uncharted stars in the galaxy, up to an amazing five billion stars for any one presentation.

A smaller exhibit is the "Big Bang," which contains a central thirty-six-foot screen over an eight-foot-deep bowl around which visitors gather, standing on Plexiglass flooring. The show uses lasers, dozens of lighting effects, an LED display, narration, and surround sound to immerse viewers in the imagery and energy of the early universe.

The Hayden Sphere also houses other exhibit halls that present phenomena such as cosmic evolution; the formation of galaxies, stars, and planets; the collision of galaxies; and the formation of a supernova.

Director of the Charles Hayden Planetarium

The Charles Hayden Planetarium is part of the Museum of Science, Boston. The planetarium uses a Zeiss Star Projector, which is a rotating star simulator that projects nine thousand stars and twenty-nine constellations onto a sixty-foot dome. Computer-generated images of planets, galaxies, and black holes are incorporated into different-themed programs.

The rooftop of the museum's garage is home to the Gilliland Observatory, which features a seven-inch refractor and a twelve-inch Schmidt-Cassegrain telescope. These instruments allow powerful views of the universe, including sunspots, stars, planets, lunar craters, and distant sky objects. The observatory can also transmit "live" pictures of space objects directly from the telescopes to the planetarium's theater.

Larry Schindler is the director of the Charles Hayden Planetarium. He earned his B.S. from the Massachusetts Institute of Technology in electrical engineering and humanities and worked in engineering before starting at the planetarium in 1967 as a lecturer/technician. At first, his time was split between fixing and making things and teaching courses and conducting live programs. Larry next moved on to become the producer and stayed in that position until he was promoted to director in 1987.

Schindler explains that the job of a planetarium is to visually portray astronomical and space science phenomena and to present programs that translate these phenomena to the general public. This is accomplished by employing a combination of media such as film, videotape, slide show, star projector, or a special-effects device to project images onto the planetarium dome.

The Charles Hayden Planetarium produces its own shows, but there are also premade packages that can be purchased. Some of the shows have been produced under grants, and some are sold by the planetariums that produce them. Show packages typically include a script, a sound track, and slides or a videotape that the purchasing facility puts together to suit its needs. This multimedia effort is operated under a central control system. Sophisticated computers run the show, which used to be managed manually with buttons and knobs. Most shows include a sound track that operates in sync with the rest of the show.

"It always requires somebody to run the show," Schindler explains. "It used to be that the presenter would be at the console where all the controls are at one edge of the planetarium—a combination podium and control board with a microphone, knobs, and buttons. But we are now getting into a presentation method where the person actually goes out in front or walks around in the audience while holding a remote control unit and conducting the program from out there.

"It takes a lot of different kinds of experience and talents to put this all together. Once you've established the content, it's a lot like producing a film or show."

Duties of the Director

Schindler describes the director's office as "a nerve center and contact for information flowing into and out of the planetarium. In the old days it was very possible to make a decision and just do it, but that doesn't hold any more. Now it involves communicating with three or four other departments—organizing meetings. That sort of thing."

Schindler's fascination with both astronomy and technology is a perfect combination in this field. He enjoys the challenge of trying to convey the excitement of the science to audiences and names getting to "play with all those wonderful toys" as one of the job's perks.

"Sometimes it's pressured, particularly in a large organization, where you have a lot of different things to tend to. But I don't think that pressure is a negative. There are odd hours; we're open seven days a week and some nights, but the people who work those hours have a certain amount of choice.

"The downside is nobody is getting rich."

Advice from Larry Schindler

Larry says that a background in astronomy is not necessary for many of the jobs in a planetarium. Much of the work can be learned on the job, but the basic interest in computers and audiovisual equipment is definitely beneficial.

The ability to deal with the variety of visitors is also important. Some planetariums focus on teaching, and employees would need to deal with students. The ability to answer questions and solve problems is a plus.

Operations Coordinator at the Charles Hayden Planetarium

Noreen Grice is operations coordinator at the Charles Hayden Planetarium at Boston's Museum of Science. She has a bachelor's degree in astronomy from Boston University and a master's in astronomy from San Diego State University.

Grice describes her position as less a researcher and more an educator and liaison between the research and the public. Her background in astronomy qualifies her to translate the research into information that can be presented to the public and to check the scientific accuracy of the scripts for the planetarium's shows.

Grice's job has included coordinating special events such as "Astronomy Day" and "Space Week." "Astronomy Day" is an international event intended to spark interest in astronomy. She invites astronomy clubs and local small planetariums to set up display tables at the museum. There are special shows to be arranged, and Grice invites speakers to give talks on different topics.

Grice is also a teacher. When she first started, the only classes offered were very specialized ones for adults. She created courses for children ranging from preschool through high school. The classes cover the earth and moon, sun and stars, and the planets. Today she is one of several instructors for many courses offered.

Part of Grice's job includes answering questions from the public and letters from schoolchildren. She initially wrote individual replies to each letter, but when it became apparent that specific questions were asked repeatedly, Grice composed fifteen brochures on different astronomy topics.

Grice's advice to anyone hoping to work in a position similar to hers is to study astronomy. In her opinion, "It would give you an edge over the competition and peace of mind knowing in your heart that what you're talking about is accurate." Astronomy will also give you the foundation to interpret the research being done in the field.

Career Outlook and Earnings

There are many planetariums throughout the United States and Canada, ranging from those as large as New York's Hayden Sphere and Toronto's Ontario Science Centre to small institutions maintained by local school districts. In any setting, it takes a number of people to keep a planetarium running. As our interest in science and space travel grows, the number of visitors to planetariums increases each year.

One good way to secure a position in a planetarium is to volunteer. Many planetariums announce job openings to other planetariums, and being present as a volunteer or intern can give you an edge in learning about new positions. You can learn about volunteer opportunities and job openings by visiting the websites of many planetariums.

The size and location of the planetarium dictates most earnings. An astronomy educator at a moderate-sized institution might earn between $35,000 and $40,000; an educator in a small regional planetarium would earn considerably less, while salaries at large institutions would be higher.

Salaries vary from institution to institution, but even in large cities, salaries are not glamorous. One recent job posting for an assistant curator at a small planetarium, requiring a bachelor's degree and one year of experience, lists an annual salary in the low twenties. Astronomers with doctoral degrees will earn higher salaries, since they are often tenured faculty members at affiliated universities. The amount of experience and education you bring to the position and your location will determine how much you earn.

Job Information Service for Planetariums

The International Planetarium Society operates a job information service. To learn more about membership benefits, links to other resources, and to view job listings, go to www.ips-planetarium.org.

9

NATIONAL HISTORIC SITES

THROUGHOUT BOTH THE United States and Canada, residents and travelers alike can visit any number of historical and recreational sites. Managed by each country's government, these sites are, in effect, museums in which we can learn a great deal about the history of the countries and their people.

National Park Service

The National Park Service, a bureau under the U.S. Department of the Interior, administers more than 160 natural and recreational areas across the country, including the Grand Canyon, Yellowstone National Park, and Lake Mead.

Another two hundred sites of cultural and historic significance fall under the Park Service's jurisdiction, and they service millions of visitors each year. These national parks, monuments, memorials, battlefields, forts, and other sites offer numerous employment opportunities of interest to museum lovers.

Here is a small selection of some of the better-known parts of the system:

Appomattox Court House, Virginia (where Lee's surrender
    to Grant ended the Civil War)
Arlington House, Robert E. Lee Memorial, Virginia
Death Valley National Monument, California
Edison National Historic Site, New Jersey (where Thomas
    Edison had his laboratory)
Ellis Island, New York
Fords Theater, Washington, DC
Frederick Douglas Home, Washington, DC
Golden Spike National Historic Site, Utah (the site where
    the first transcontinental railroad lines met)
Independence Hall, Philadelphia
John F. Kennedy Center, Washington, DC
Liberty Bell, Philadelphia
Lincoln Memorial, Washington, DC
Mount Rushmore National Memorial, South Dakota
Statue of Liberty National Monument, New York
Teddy Roosevelt Birthplace, New York
White House, Washington, DC

St. Augustine, Florida

St. Augustine, Florida, is America's oldest city. Viewed from the air or from the Bridge of Lions (named for the Spanish explorer Ponce de Leon), the city resembles a European burg or medieval hamlet. Fairy-tale castles with spires and turrets rise above the roofs of the gingerbread-trimmed dollhouses. Horse-drawn carriages, stone walls, city gates, and an old fort add to the fanciful effect.

Reputedly one of the oldest roadways in the oldest city in the country, St. George Street was fully restored in the midseventies. On either side of the narrow promenade, buildings bear signs proclaiming the "Oldest Wooden School House" (built during the first Spanish occupation before the American Revolution), the "Oldest Pharmacy," and the "Oldest Store," with a collection of more than one hundred thousand of yesterday's mementos.

St. Augustine's "Oldest House," originally built with palm thatchings covering a crude structure of logs and boards, then restored after a fire in 1702 with coquina walls and *tapia* flooring (a mixture of lime, shell, and sand), is one of the most-studied and best-documented houses in the United States. It provides a record of life in St. Augustine for more than four hundred years. In spite of raids, looting, and fire, archaeologists have shown through digs and research that the site has been continuously occupied from the early 1600s to the present.

Nearby, the Authentic Old Jail, listed in the National Register of Historic Places, contains the original weapons used in crimes and offers an interesting courtyard display. The building, with living quarters for the sheriff and his family, served the county until 1953.

South of the Old City Gate is St. Augustine's Spanish Quarter. This area is a living history museum that includes restored homes and gardens that are more than 250 years old. Guides and craftspeople dressed in period clothing re-create the daily lifestyle, giving visitors an inside look at the lives of eighteenth-century soldiers and settlers.

Castillo de San Marcos National Monument, built by the Spanish between 1672 and 1695 and now run by the National Park Service, is America's oldest fort. It took more than fifty years after Ponce de Leon claimed La Florida for Spain to establish a permanent settlement in St. Augustine. The early Spaniards had many clashes with colonialists in neighboring Georgia and the Carolinas. St. Augustine was burned to the ground twice. The fort was constructed to secure the city. Lacking brick-making materials, the Spanish used *coquina* blocks, a native shell-stone quarried locally across the bay on Anastasia Island. Softer than brick, which would shatter upon strong impact, coquina helped the fort withstand numerous attacks by absorbing the impact of iron cannon balls.

The coquina (Spanish for "shells") tends to break off when touched and portions of the fort have eroded away. The damage is irreparable; a mortar substitute could be used to patch the surface in places, but park rangers warn visitors not to lean against the walls.

The fort raised different flags above its walls many times over the years, through wartime and peace, through treaties, trades, and negotiations, but in 1821 it changed hands for the last time when the United States acquired Florida from Spain. (The fort is also significant in that it houses the nation's oldest toilets.)

Park Rangers (Interpretation)

The National Park Service hires three categories of park rangers (generally on a seasonal basis): enforcement, general, and interpretation. Most people interested in museum work apply for positions in the interpretation category.

Duties vary greatly from position to position and from site to site, but rangers in the interpretation division are usually responsible for developing and presenting programs that explain a park's historic, cultural, or archaeological features. This is done through talks, demonstrations, and guided walking tours. Rangers also sit at information desks, provide visitor services, or participate in conservation or restoration projects. Entry-level employees might also collect fees, administer first aid, and operate audiovisual equipment.

How to Apply for a Job

Recruitment for summer employment with the National Park Service begins September 1 with a January 15 deadline. Some sites, such as Death Valley or Everglades National Park, also have a busy winter season. The winter recruitment period occurs June 1 through July 15.

Applications for seasonal employment with the National Park Service can be obtained through the Office of Personnel Management or by writing to the U.S. Department of the Interior, National Park Service, Seasonal Employment Unit, P.O. Box 37127, Washington, DC 20013-7127. You can also contact one of the nine regional offices of the National Park Service. Its addresses are listed in Appendix D.

Competition for park ranger jobs, especially at the most well-known sites, can be extremely fierce. The National Park Service already employs a large staff of permanent rangers, which is supplemented by a seasonal workforce in peak visitation periods during the summer and school breaks.

In light of this stiff competition, one of the best ways to secure a position is by working during school vacations as a seasonal employee. The National Park Service looks favorably on applicants for permanent positions who have worked for the service one or more summer seasons. In addition, veterans of the U.S. Armed Forces may be given preference among applicants, depending on their experience.

Qualifications and Salaries

The National Park Service weighs several factors when determining a candidate's eligibility for employment and at which salary level he or she will be placed. In general, those with the least experience or education will begin at the lowest federal government salary grade of GS-2. The requirements for the GS-2 grade are six months' experience in related work or a high school diploma or its equivalent.

The more related work experience or education an applicant has, the higher the salary level. For example, GS-4 requires eighteen months of general experience in park operations or in related fields and six months of specialized experience; or one ninety-day season as a seasonal park ranger at the GS-3 level.

Completion of two academic years of college may be substituted for experience if the course work covered is related to the duties of a park ranger.

Superintendent at Castillo de San Marcos National Monument

Gordie Wilson graduated from college in 1977 with a degree in parks and recreation and immediately began working for the National Park Service. Today, in addition to his post as superintendent of Castillo de San Marcos, he is also in charge of nearby Fort Matanzas National Monument.

Wilson talks about how a park ranger does not generally have a typical day. He says, "Duties are varied and there is always the unexpected." In any given day, a park ranger might work at a ticket booth collecting fees, give a two-hour presentation to visitors, set off cannons in a daily display (in period costume), and ensure that visitors are not damaging the property in any way. Rangers are also trained in CPR to assist visitors in need of medical attention.

Interpretive Ranger at Ellis Island

Tom Bernardin is an interpretive ranger at Ellis Island, the point through which many immigrants entered the United States. A former teacher of English as a second language, Bernardin hoped to get a job on the maintenance staff at the Statue of Liberty; he wanted to cut grass. When the woman who interviewed him realized his qualifications, she suggested that he join her interpretive staff. Bernardin was aware of the position, but was hesitant because his only public speaking experience was from teaching, and he was nervous. Fortunately, he was able to put his doubts aside. As Bernardin says, "I took the job and had absolutely no regrets."

Bernardin worked as a seasonal employee (from April through October) for three years in the early days of the museum, which opened in 1975. As a park ranger and member of the interpretive staff, he put in eight hours a day, five days a week. Before he conducted his first tour, he underwent a two-week training program given in a boardroom at the base of the Statue of Liberty. In addition to learning about general park regulations, Bernardin was given a list of books to read and absorbed everything he could about the history of Ellis Island.

Ellis Island is part of the Statue of Liberty National Monument, which rangers reach by taking a staff boat that leaves from lower Manhattan at 8:30 each morning. The rangers arrive on the island in time to change into uniform and greet visitors from the first tour boat of the day at 9:15.

Bernardin explains that each boat holds up to 150 people, but on some days hardly any visitors show up. On those days the rangers are free to explore the thirty-two buildings on the island, many of which are not open to the public. Some days the visitors include groups of schoolchildren. Sundays are the busiest days, with up to seven full boats arriving throughout the day.

The rangers work with a planned tour route, and each boatload of visitors gets its own individual tour. Bernardin says, "So, it's Sunday, it's summer, and it's a beautiful day and 150 people from Manhattan pull up. That requires a lot of rangers—about seven. I used to beg for that tour."

Bernardin enjoyed the feeling he got standing on a flight of steps above the crowd outside the main building and relating the history of the site. Next he would lead the group into the baggage room, which is where the immigrants' bags were inspected. He would talk about the journey across the ocean and then take everyone into the Great Hall, which is one of the most famous parts of the museum. It is here that visitors can have the often emotional experience of sitting on the benches where the immigrants sat and waited. Bernardin would ask whether any of the visitors had come through Ellis Island as immigrants themselves; if any had, he would encourage them to tell their story to the group.

Throughout the tour, Bernardin discussed immigration history, pointing out the various aspects of the immigrants' experience in different parts of the museum. After the initial tour through the larger areas, the group is divided into three smaller groups and taken by various rangers through the social services room, the legal room, and the old dining room. These groups are led by an interpretive ranger assisted by a back-up ranger.

Running extensive tours requires coordination, as rangers must try to keep the different groups from running into one another along the way. An extra ranger floats among the groups to keep things moving smoothly. At the end of the day, rangers change out of their uniforms and take the last boat back with the visitors.

Bernardin enjoyed his time as an interpretive ranger. "The best part of my job was having access to Ellis Island and becoming a part of its history, making the public aware of how important it was, tapping into the emotions visitors brought with them."

It has been more than two decades since Bernardin left his job at Ellis Island, but the monument is still with him. In 1981 he developed a slide lecture called "Ellis Island: The Golden Door," and in 1991 published *The Ellis Island Immigrant Cookbook*. In addition to the recipes contributed by immigrants and their descendants, there are heart-warming, and at times heart-wrenching, accounts of the Ellis Island experience. Bernardin regularly tours the country speaking to different groups about the rich history of Ellis Island.

Parks Canada Wardens

Throughout Canada, national parks, historic sites, marine conservation areas, and historic canals are maintained to protect their representation of the natural and marine regions of the country, particularly those that reflect Canada's cultural diversity. Parks Canada is the government agency that oversees these national sites.

Canada's national park system started in 1885 with the establishment of Banff National Park in Alberta. Since that time, the total area of Canada's parks has expanded to about 69,498 square miles, including thirty-two national parks and eighty national historic parks and sites. The national historic parks preserve such features as forts, monuments, houses, canals, and trails.

Here is a small sample of Canada's national treasures:

Alexander Graham Bell National Historic Site, Nova Scotia
Batoche National Historic Site, Saskatchewan

Fort Walsh, Saskatchewan
Laurier's House, Ottawa
Sir John Johnson's House, Toronto
Woodside National Historic Site, Ontario

Parks Canada employs approximately four hundred park wardens, whose responsibilities include protecting and managing natural resources, providing scientific information, and administering public safety programs.

Park wardens work in a variety of national parks or historic sites across the country. Their work environment varies depending on the location of the site. Regardless of where a park warden works, he or she will most likely live in a small community in or adjacent to the park, since very few national parks are near large cities.

Park wardens interact with the local people and organizations that are involved in the management and operation of the park. They work with local people who have an intimate knowledge of the park area and its resources based on personal experiences and generations of traditional knowledge. This knowledge and experience is valuable and a consideration in the management of the park.

Qualifications and Training

The minimum educational requirement to become a park warden is a university degree in the sciences or natural resources. The park warden's duties require a good level of physical fitness and the ability to travel and work in a variety of terrestrial and marine environments. Experience in wilderness travel using a variety of personal and technical equipment and techniques (such as hiking, canoeing, snowmobiling, and so forth) is required. Additional requirements include hands-on experience in natural resource management, public safety, or building community relationships. Although park wardens often live in secluded settings, they must be able to establish partnerships and communicate and interact effectively with a variety of people.

Other basic qualifications include a valid driver's license, valid first-aid and CPR certificates, a pleasure-craft operator license, and successful completion of a Canadian firearms safety course. A pre-employment medical exam and a security check are also required.

Parks Canada Opportunities for Students

Each year, Parks Canada offers more than one thousand jobs to full-time students in secondary schools, colleges, technical institutes, and universities. These jobs generally run from May to September and are available in the warden service, visitor services, assistance on the waterways, interpretive activities, systems work, and office support.

These summer jobs afford students the opportunity to learn about Parks Canada and the federal government. Students also gain valuable work experience and learn skills to improve their future employment prospects.

To be eligible for summer employment, students must meet the following criteria: be a full-time secondary or postsecondary student in an accredited institution, plan to return to full-time studies in the next academic term, and be of the minimum age to work in the province where the job is located.

Students who have worked for Parks Canada are often rehired the following summer by the same park or site. To be considered for reemployment, students must continue to meet the eligibility criteria and have worked in a student job with Parks Canada within the past year.

Compensation for student jobs is based on rates established by Parks Canada in keeping with federal government student programs. If travel and accommodation expenses are incurred, they are paid by the agency.

10

ARCHIVES AND GENEALOGY

ARCHIVISTS AND GENEALOGISTS are professionals who deal with the past. In a museum setting, both archivists and genealogists use various methods to research and catalog the past. In this chapter we examine both fields.

Archives

Archives hold firsthand information, so they are valuable to anyone with an interest in the people, places, and events of the past. Genealogists, researchers, scholars, students, writers, and historians are among the vast number of people whose work can be enhanced by using archives.

The exact number is not known, but it's estimated that there are several thousand archives in North America. More than five thousand archives exist in the United States—each of the fifty states maintains a government archive, as do most city and county governments. The same types of archives are kept in Canada. Archives are also found in universities, historical societies, museums, libraries, and private businesses.

On the national level there is the National Archives in Washington, DC, which looks after the records of the federal government. The Library of Congress provides information services to the U.S. Congress and technical services to all the libraries in the country.

Library and Archives Canada, the federal archive of Canada, combines the services of the former National Library and National Archive.

Although archives are similar to libraries, there are distinct differences between the two. Libraries typically house materials that are published and were created with the express purpose of broad dissemination. Archives typically hold materials that were created in the course of some business or activity but were never intended originally for public use. For example, an archive might include letters from a Civil War soldier to his family. He wrote about his experiences and feelings and to let his loved ones know that he was still alive. He never would have imagined that his correspondence would one day appear in an archive. Inclusion in an archive gives his letters credibility and integrity as a historical source.

Archives handle collections that chart the course of daily life for individuals and businesses. Some archives specifically look after materials created by their own institutions. The Coca-Cola Company, for example, set up an archive years ago so that it could have a history of what the company business was and how it prospered. New companies set up archives to keep a documented record of their business.

Educational institutions such as universities or museums create archives that relate to their special research interests.

The material found in an archive can include letters, personal papers, and organizational records. Archives created within the last one hundred years or so can also contain visual records, such as photographs, postcards, prints, drawings, and sketches. Today archives also contain phonograph records, audiotapes, videotapes, movie films, and computer-stored information.

Archivists

As with libraries and archives, there are distinct differences between librarians and archivists, including the way they operate and the methods and techniques they use to handle material.

The greatest difference is that librarians took at materials they get on an item-by-item basis. Each book is a distinct entity evaluated separately from the other books. In an archive, on the other hand, a single letter would usually be part of a larger collection of letters. Archivists are interested in these as a group because one letter would only be a fragment. To really understand something about the past, the information needs to be synthesized and put together in a collection.

When archivists talk about their work, they discuss certain basic functions that are common to all archives. The numbers following the five areas below designate the percentage of time usually spent with each duty.

Arrangement and description of collections	60%
Identification and acquisition of materials	10%
Preservation of collections	10%
Reference services	15%
Community outreach and public affairs	5%

The information that archivists collect, organize, and control takes many forms. Working in accordance with accepted standards and practices, archivists maintain these records to ensure their long-term preservation and easy retrieval.

Original records maintained by archivists can take many forms, such as photographs, films, video and sound recordings, computer tapes, and video and optical disks, as well as more traditional paper records, letters, and documents. They also may be copied onto some other format to protect the original and to make them more accessible to researchers who use the records. As various storage media evolve, archivists must keep abreast of technological advances in electronic information storage.

Archivists often specialize in an area of history or technology so they can more accurately determine what records in that area qualify for retention and should become part of the archives. They may also work with specialized forms of records, such as manuscripts, electronic records, photographs, cartographic records, motion pictures, and sound recordings.

Computers are increasingly being used to generate and maintain archival records. Professional standards for the use of computers in handling archival records are still evolving. However, computers are expected to transform many aspects of archival collections as computer capabilities and the use of multimedia and the Internet expand and allow more records to be stored and exhibited electronically.

Working Conditions

Working conditions of archivists vary. Some might spend most of their time working with the public providing reference assistance and educational services; others might perform research or process records, which often means working alone or in offices with few people.

Qualifications and Training

People get into the archives profession in a variety of traditional and unusual ways. Often in a small town, an archive is a closet in the back room of a local historical society's office. Someone volunteers to put it all together, thus becoming the keeper of the community's history—or its archivist.

In more traditional settings, employment as an archivist usually requires graduate education and related work experience. While completing their formal education, many archivists and curators work in archives or museums to gain the hands-on experience that many employers seek.

Although several undergraduate degrees are acceptable, most employers prefer a graduate degree in history or library science, with courses in archival science. Some positions may require knowledge of the discipline related to the collection, such as business or medicine, for example.

There are approximately sixty-five colleges and universities that offer courses or practical training in archival science as part of history, library science, or another discipline. At this time, there are no schools in the United States that offer a distinct master of archival studies degree. There are schools in Canada that offer the degree, which has been established according to guidelines set by the Association of Canadian Archivists.

Certification

The Academy of Certified Archivists offers voluntary certification for archivists. The designation "Certified Archivist" is obtained by those with at least a master's degree and a year of appropriate archival experience. The certification process requires candidates to pass a written examination, and they must periodically renew their certification.

Desirable Traits and Skills

Archivists need research and analytical ability to understand the content of documents and the context in which they were created and to decipher deteriorated or poor-quality printed matter, hand-written manuscripts, or photographs and films. A background in preservation management is often required of archivists because they are responsible for taking proper care of their records.

Archivists also must be able to organize large amounts of information and write clear instructions for its retrieval and use. In addition, computer skills and the ability to work with electronic records and databases are becoming increasingly important.

Employment of Archivists

Archivists, along with curators and museum technicians, held about twenty-seven thousand jobs in 2004. The majority worked in federal, state, and local government archives, followed by those who were employed in museums, historical sites, and similar institutions. A smaller percentage worked for state and private educational institutions, mainly college and university libraries. The rest were employed in industry or by private archives.

Most federal archivists work for the National Archives and Records Administration; others manage military archives in the U.S. Department of Defense. Most federal government curators work at the Smithsonian Institution, in the military museums of the Department of Defense, and in archaeological and other museums and historic sites managed by the U.S. Department of the Interior. All state governments have archival or historical-record sections employing archivists. State and local governments also have numerous historical museums, parks, libraries, and zoos employing curators.

Some large corporations that have archives or record centers employ archivists to manage the growing volume of records created or maintained as required by law or necessary to the firms' operations. Religious and fraternal organizations, professional associations, conservation organizations, major private collectors, and research firms also employ archivists and curators.

Job Outlook for Archivists

Competition for jobs as archivists is expected to be strong because qualified applicants outnumber job openings. The best opportunities should be for graduates with highly specialized training, such as master's degrees in both library science and history, with a concentration in archives or records management and extensive computer skills.

Employment of archivists is expected to increase about as fast as the average for all occupations through 2012. Jobs are expected to grow as public and private organizations emphasize establishing archives and organizing records and information and as public interest in science, art, history, and technology increases.

Museum and zoo attendance has been on the rise and is expected to continue increasing; however, museums and other cultural institutions can be subject to cuts in funding during recessions or periods of budget tightening, reducing demand for archivists.

Although the rate of turnover among archivists is relatively low, the need to replace workers who leave the occupation or stop working will create job openings. Archivists typically advance by transferring to a larger unit with supervisory positions. A doctorate in history, library science, or a related field may be needed for some advanced positions, such as director of a state archive.

Earnings

Earnings of archivists vary considerably by type and size of employer and often by specialty. Median annual earnings of archivists were $36,470 in 2004. The middle 50 percent earned between $28,900 and $46,480. The lowest 10 percent earned less than $21,780, and the highest 10 percent earned more than $61,260.

The average annual salary for archivists in the federal government in nonsupervisory, supervisory, and managerial positions was $75,876 in 2005; for museum curators, $76,126; for museum specialists and technicians, $55,291; and for archives technicians, $41,347.

Chief Archivist at the National Museum of American History

John Fleckner is the chief archivist at the Smithsonian Institution's National Museum of American History. He came to the Smithsonian in 1982 with more than a decade's experience working as an archivist for the State Historical Society of Wisconsin. He is a past president of the Society of American Archivists and has acted as a consultant on many important archives projects, including the United Negro College Fund, the Viet Nam History and Archives Project, and the Native American Archives Project.

Fleckner did his undergraduate work at Colgate University, in Hamilton, New York, graduating with a B.A. with honors in history. He earned his master's degree in American history at the University of Wisconsin.

Fleckner's initial interest was not in a career as an archivist. His original plan was to teach college-level history, until a university career counselor pointed him toward a graduate program in archives administration. At the time this seemed like a more profitable career choice, and John decided to pursue it.

Once Fleckner began doing archival work, he realized how much he enjoyed it. As he says, "I loved the intense, intimate contact with the 'stuff' of history. Before I completed my internship, I knew I wanted to be an archivist." During his own research as a graduate student, archived material had seemed antiseptic and lifeless. Once he became an archivist, though, he found the materials thrilling and loved "the mystery, the possibilities of the records themselves."

The Archivist's Duties

The archive Fleckner is responsible for acquires collections from the outside and does not handle the records generated by the museum. The collections cover a wide range of subjects and are particularly strong in the areas of American music, advertising, and the history of technology. Fleckner oversees a professional staff of twelve archivists, three student interns, and close to twenty volunteers.

As an archivist, Fleckner makes decisions that will determine how future researchers access the records. In a sense, he gets to reconstruct the past and to imagine the future through the records he handles. Fleckner follows established techniques and methods and maintains standards against which his work is judged.

Genealogists

The study of genealogy, which is the tracing family histories, in addition to being one of the most popular hobbies in the United

States is also a profession valued by many archives as well as history and living history museums. To accurately document the lives of people from a particular time period, the services of genealogists are used in addition to those of more general researchers.

Genealogists also are employed in historical societies and libraries with special genealogy rooms. The Church of Jesus Christ of Latter-Day Saints in Salt Lake City, for example, maintains a huge repository of family information in its Family History Library. It employs genealogists all over the world or includes genealogists who have been accredited through their own program on a list of freelance researchers. Go to www.familysearch.org for more information.

Other genealogists find work teaching their skills in adult education classes, editing genealogy magazines, or writing books or newspaper genealogy columns.

Training and Certification

Although many genealogists are not formally trained, specializing in genealogy is possible through some university history and library science programs. And even though there is not a specified curriculum for genealogists, the Board for Certification of Genealogists stresses the importance of certification for those interested in seriously pursuing this field. Detailed information about certification is available from the Board for Certification of Genealogists at www.bcgcertification.org.

The National Genealogical Society in Arlington, Virginia, and Brigham Young University in Provo, Utah, offer independent study courses. The National Institute on Genealogical Research in Washington, DC, and Samford University Institute of Genealogy and

Historical Research in Birmingham, Alabama, both offer intensive five-day programs covering various aspects of genealogy.

In addition, many local and state genealogy societies sponsor one- and two-day seminars. Information about these seminars is published in the newsletters of both the Federation of Genealogical Societies and the National Genealogical Society. These organizations also hold annual conferences at various sites nationwide. Information about useful publications and conferences is available on their websites at www.fgs.org and www.ngsgenealogy.org.

How to Get Started

One of the nice things about genealogy is that you can pursue it on your own before making a commitment to serious study. In this way you can decide whether this is the right type of career for you.

The National Genealogical Society suggests beginning with your own family tree as an introduction to genealogy and offers the following suggestions for how to get started:

- **Make a chart.** Begin with you, your parents, grandparents, and great-grandparents. This will be the beginning of your family tree.
- **Search for records.** Look for birth, marriage, and death certificates and any other documents that might provide names, dates, and locations. Check your family's Bible records, old letters, and photographs for clues to people's identities and relationships. Label everything you find to make it easier to organize your research.
- **Talk to family members.** Encourage older relatives to talk about their childhoods and relatives and listen carefully for

clues they might inadvertently drop. Learn good interviewing techniques so you can ask questions that elicit the most productive answers. Use a tape recorder or camcorder, and try to verify each fact through a separate source.

- **Visit the local library.** Become familiar with historical and genealogical publications and contact local historical societies. Check out the state library and the archives in your state capital. Seek out any specialty ethnic or religious libraries, and visit cemeteries.
- **Visit courthouses.** Cultivate friendships with busy court clerks. Ask to see source records such as wills, deeds, marriage books, and birth and death certificates that are not readily available from family members.
- **Enter into correspondence.** Write to other individuals or societies involved with the same families or regions. Contact foreign embassies in Washington, DC. Restrict yourself to asking only one question in each letter you send. Include the information you have already uncovered. Include a self-addressed stamped envelope and your e-mail address to encourage replies.
- **Use the Internet.** Many public records are available on the Internet. In addition, there are websites designed specifically for genealogical research. Some sites offer full access only to those who pay a registration fee; some offer software that allows you to keep track of your research. Two popular sites are www.genealogy.com and www.ancestry.com.
- **Keep painstaking records.** Use printed family group sheets or pedigree charts. Develop a well-organized filing system so you'll be able to easily find your information. Enter your

research information into a database if possible. Keep separate records for each family you research.

- **Contact the National Genealogical Society.** Browse its online bookstore for helpful publications. You can enroll in its home study course titled "American Genealogy: A Basic Course," or you can take a course through its online learning center. The website is www.ngsgeanealogy.org.

Salaries for Genealogists

According to the Society of Professional Genealogists, most genealogical practices charge by the hour and also bill for out-of-pocket expenses such as photocopies, telephone calls, travel, and vital records fees. Hourly rates range from about $15 to $100, with the average between $25 and $60. Fees vary among professionals, depending upon experience, credentials, specialty, and geographic area. Highly skilled experts who specialize in unusually difficult research problems may charge higher rates.

Appendix A

Professional Associations

The following list of associations can be used as a valuable resource guide in locating additional information about specific careers. Many of the organizations publish newsletters that list job and internship opportunities; others offer an employment service to members. A quick look at the organizations' names will give you an idea of how large a scope the museums cover.

National Associations

Advisory Council on Historic Preservation
1100 Pennsylvania Ave. NW, Ste. 809
Washington, DC 20004
www.achp.gov

American Anthropological Association
2200 Wilson Blvd., Ste. 600
Arlington, VA 22201
www.aaanet.org

American Arts Alliance
1112 16th St. NW, Ste. 400
Washington, DC 20036
www.americanartsalliance.org

American Association for the Advancement of Science
1200 New York Ave. NW
Washington, DC 20005
www.aaas.org

American Association of Botanical Gardens and Arboreta
100 W. 10th St., Ste. 614
Wilmington, DE 19801
www.aabga.org

American Association for Museum Volunteers
www.acnatsci.org/hosted/aamv/index.htm

American Association of Museums
1575 Eye St. NW, Ste. 400
Washington, DC 20005
www.aam-us.org

American Association for State and Local History
1717 Church St.
Nashville, TN 37203-2991
www.aaslh.org

American Craft Council
72 Spring St.
New York, NY 10012-4019
www.craftcouncil.org

American Historical Association
400 A St. SE
Washington, DC 20003-3889
www.historians.org

American Institute of Architects
1735 New York Ave. NW
Washington, DC 20006-5292
www.aia.org

American Institute for Conservation of Historic and Artistic Works
1717 K St. NW, Ste. 200
Washington, DC 20036-5346
www.aic.stanford.edu

American Library Association
50 E. Huron St.
Chicago, IL 60611
www.ala.org

American Society of Interior Designers
608 Massachusetts Ave. NE
Washington, DC 20002-6006
www.asid.org

American Society of Landscape Architects
636 Eye St. NW
Washington, DC 20001-3736
www.asla.org

American Zoo and Aquarium Association
8403 Colesville Rd., Ste. 710
Silver Spring, MD 20910
www.aza.org

Archaeological Conservancy
5301 Central Ave. NE, Ste. 1218
Albuquerque, NM 87108-1517
www.americanarchaeology.com

Archaeological Institute of America
656 Beacon St., 4th Fl.
Boston, MA 02115-2006
www.archaeological.org

Archives of American Art
Smithsonian Institution
P.O. Box 37012
Victor Bldg., Rm. 2200, MRC 937
Washington, DC 20013-7012
www.aaa.si.edu

Art Dealers Association of America
575 Madison Ave.
New York, NY 10022
www.artdealers.org

Association of African-American Museums
P.O. Box 578
1350 Brush Row Rd.
Wilberforce, OH 45384
www.blackmuseums.org

Association of Art Museum Directors
41 E. 65th St.
New York, NY 10021
www.aamd.org

Association of Children's Museums
1300 L St. NW, #975
Washington, DC 20005
www.childrensmuseums.org

Association of College and University Museums and Galleries
601 E. Main St.
Collegeville, PA 19426
www.acumg.org

Association for Gravestone Studies
278 Main St., Ste. 207
Greenfield, MA 01301
www.gravestonestudies.org

Association for Living History, Farm, and Agricultural Museums
8774 Route 45 NW
North Bloomfield, OH 44450
www.alhfam.org

Association for Preservation Technology International
4513 Lincoln Ave., Ste. 213
Lisle, IL 60532-1290
www.apti.org

Association of Railway Museums
P.O. Box 370
Tujunga, CA 91043-0370
www.railwaymuseums.org

Association of Science-Technology Centers
1025 Vermont Ave. NW, Ste. 500
Washington, DC 20005-6310
www.astc.org

Astronomical League
9201 Ward Pkwy., Ste. #100
Kansas City, MO 64114
www.astroleague.org

Canadian Art Museums Directors Organization
280 Metcalfe St., Ste. 400
Ottawa, ON K2P 1R7
www.museums.ca

Canadian Association of Science Centres
100 Ramsey Lake Rd.
Sudbury, ON P3E 5S9
www.canadiansciencecentres.ca

Canadian Museums Association
280 Metcalfe St., Ste. 400
Ottawa, ON K2P 1R7
www.museums.ca

Costume Society of America
P.O. Box 73
Earleville, MD 21919
www.costumesocietyamerica.com

Council of American Jewish Museums
The National Foundation for Jewish Culture
330 7th Ave., 21st Fl.
New York, NY 10001
www2.jewishculture.org/cultural_services/museums/cajm

Council of American Maritime Museums
www.councilofamericanmaritimemuseums.org

Council for Museum Anthropology
2200 Wilson Blvd., Ste. 600
Arlington, VA 22201
www.nmnh.si.edu/anthro/cma/index.html

Federation of Genealogical Societies
P.O. Box 200940
Austin, TX 78720
www.fgs.org

Genealogical Library
Church of Jesus Christ of Latter-day Saints
Family History Library
35 North West Temple St.
Salt Lake City, UT 84150-3400
www.familysearch.org

Heritage Preservation (National Institute for Conservation)
1012 14th St. NW, Ste. 1200
Washington, DC 20005
www.heritagepreservation.org

International Council on Monuments and Sites
Canadian National Committee
P.O. Box 737, Station B
Ottawa, ON K1P 5P8
http://canada.icomos.org

International Council on Monuments and Sites
U.S. Committee
401 F St. NW, Ste. 331
Washington, DC 20001
www.icomos.org/usicomos

International Museum Theater Alliance
The Putnam Museum
1717 W. 12th St.
Davenport, IA 52804
www.imtal.org

International Planetarium Society
P.O. Box 1812
Greenville, NC 27835
www.ips-planetarium.org

Medical Museums Association
Dittrick Medical History Center
11000 Euclid Ave.
Cleveland, OH 44106
www.case.edu/affil/MeMA/memahome.htm

Museum Computer Network
232-329 March Rd.
Box 11
Ottawa, ON K2K 2E1
www.mcn.edu

Museum Education Roundtable
621 Pennsylvania Ave. SE
Washington, DC 20003
www.mer-online.org

Museum Store Association
4100 E. Mississippi Ave., Ste. 800
Denver, CO 80246-3055
www.museumdistrict.com

National Archives and Records Administration
8601 Adelphi Rd.
College Park, MD 20740-6001
www.archives.gov

National Assembly of State Arts Agencies
1029 Vermont Ave. NW, 2nd Fl.
Washington, DC 20005
www.nasaa-arts.org

National Association of Government Archives and Records
  Administrators
90 State St., Ste. 1009
Albany, NY 12207
www.nagara.org

National Association for Interpretation
P.O. Box 2246
Fort Collins, CO 80522
www.interpretnet.com

National Genealogical Society
3108 Columbia Pike, Ste. 300
Arlington, VA 22204-4304
www.ngsgenealogy.org

National Register of Historic Places
National Park Service
1201 Eye St. NW, 8th Fl.
Washington, DC 20005
www.cr.nps.gov

National Trust for Historic Preservation
1785 Massachusetts Ave. NW
Washington, DC 20036-2117
www.nationaltrust.org

Oral History Association
Dickinson College
P.O. Box 1773
Carlisle, PA 17013
http://omega.dickinson.edu/organizations/oha

Organization of American Historians
112 N. Bryan Ave.
P.O. Box 5457
Bloomington, IN 47408
www.oah.org

Organization of Military Museums of Canada
P.O. Box 323
Gloucester, ON K1C 1S7
http://ommc.ca

Popular Culture Association
310 Auditorium Bldg.
Michigan State University
East Lansing, MI 48824
www.h-net.org

Society for American Archaeology
900 2nd St. NE, #12
Washington, DC 20002-3560
www.saa.org

Society of American Archivists
527 S. Wells St., 5th Fl.
Chicago, IL 60607
www.archivists.org

Society of American Historians
400 A St. SE
Washington, DC 20003-3889
www.historians.org

Society of Architectural Historians
1365 N. Astor St.
Chicago, IL 60610-2144
www.sah.org

Society of Systematic Biologists
1313 Dolley Madison Blvd., Ste. 402
McLean, VA 22101
http://systbio.org

Space Week International Association
14523 Sun Harbour Dr.
Houston, TX 77062
www.spaceweek.org

Urban History Association
Department of History
University of Dayton
300 College Park
Dayton, OH 45469-1540
http://uha.udayton.edu/index.htm

U.S. Census Bureau
U.S. Department of Commerce
1401 Constitution Ave. NW
Washington, DC 20230
www.census.gov

Victorian Society in America
205 S. Camac St.
Philadelphia, PA 19107
www.victoriansociety.org

World Monuments Fund
95 Madison Ave., 9th Fl.
New York, NY 10016
www.wmf.org

Regional Museum Associations

Association of Midwest Museums
P.O. Box 11940
St. Louis, MO 63112-0040
www.midwestmuseums.org

Mid-Atlantic Association of Museums
800 E. Lombard St.
Baltimore, MD 21202
www.midatlanticmuseums.org

Mountain-Plains Museum Association
7110 W. David Dr.
Littleton, CO 80128-5405
www.mountplainsmuseums.org

New England Museum Association
22 Mill St., Ste. 409
Arlington, MA 02476
www.nemanet.org

Southeastern Museums Conference
P.O. Box 9033
Atlanta, GA 31106
www.scmcdirect.nct

Western Museums Association
2960 San Pablo Ave.
Berkeley, CA 94702
www.westmuse.org

Conservation Degree and Internship Training Programs

The following symbols designate the level of training the following conservation training programs offer:

U—Undergraduate
G—Graduate
P—Postgraduate
I—Internships
C—Courses

Buffalo State College (G)
Art Conservation Department
230 Rockwell Hall
1300 Elmwood Ave.
Buffalo, NY 14222
www.buffalostate.edu/depts/artconservation

Campbell Center for Historic Preservation Studies (C)
203 E. Seminary
Mount Carroll, IL 61053
www.campbellcenter.org

Canadian Conservation Institute (G, P, I)
1030 Innes Rd.
Ottawa, ON K1A 0M5
www.cci-icc.gc.ca

Columbia University (G)
Graduate School of Architecture, Planning, and Preservation
400 Avery Hall
New York, NY 10027
www.arch.columbia.edu

Getty Conservation Institute (C)
1200 Getty Center Dr.
Los Angeles, CA 90049–1679
www.getty.edu/conservation/institute

Harvard University Art Museums (P, I)
Straus Center for Conservation and Technical Studies Training
    Program
32 Quincy St.
Cambridge, MA 02138
www.artmuseums.harvard.edu/information/internstraus.html

New York University (G)
Institute of Fine Arts
The Stephen Chan House
14 E. 78th St.
New York, NY 10021
www.nyu.edu/gsas/dept/fineart/ifa/index_chan.htm

Queens University (G)
Art Conservation Program
Department of Art
Ontario Hall
Kingston, ON K7L 3N6
www.queensu.ca/art/programs_artc.html

Smithsonian Institution (I, C)
Center for Materials Research and Education
Museum Support Center
4210 Silver Hill Rd.
Suitland, MD 20746
www.si.edu/scmre/index.asp

University of Delaware (U, G, P)
Winterthur Program in Art Conservation
303 Old College
Newark, DE 19716-2515
www.udel.edu/artcons

University of Denver (U)
School of Art and Art History
2121 E. Asbury Ave.
Denver, CO 80208
www.du.edu/art

University of Pennsylvania (G)
PennDesign
Historic Preservation Department
102 Meyerson Hall
210 S. 34th St.
Philadelphia, PA 19104-6311
www.design.upenn.edu

University of Texas at Austin (G, P)
Kilgarlin Center for Preservation of the Cultural Record
School of Information
1 University Station D7000
Austin, TX 78712
www.ischool.utexas.edu/kilgarlin

Appendix C

Addresses of Profiled Institutions

Carnegie Museum of Natural History
4400 Forbes Ave.
Pittsburgh, PA 15213-4080
www.carnegiemnh.org

Carone Gallery
600 SE Second Ct.
Fort Lauderdale, FL 33301

Castillo de San Marcos National Monument
1 Castillo Dr. East
St. Augustine, FL 32084
www.nps.gov/casa

Charles Hayden Planetarium
Museum of Science
Science Park
Boston, MA 02114
www.mos.org

Colonial Williamsburg Foundation
P.O. Box 1776
Williamsburg, VA 23187-1776
www.history.org

Ellis Island Immigration Museum
New York, NY 10004
www.ellisisland.com

Joseph Smith Historic Center
P.O. Box 365
Nauvoo, IL 62354
http://mission2mormons.org

Metropolitan Museum of Art
1000 5th Ave.
New York, NY 10028
www.metmuseum.org

Museum of Discovery and Science
401 SW 2nd St.
Ft. Lauderdale, FL 33312
www.mods.org

Museum of Fine Arts, Boston
465 Huntington Ave.
Boston, MA 02115
www.mfa.org

Museum of Science, Boston
Science Park
Boston, MA 02114
www.mos.org

Museum of Science and Industry
57th St. and Lakeshore Dr.
Chicago, IL 60637
www.msichicago.org

Nantucket Historical Association
15 Broad St.
P.O. Box 1016
Nantucket, MA 02554
www.nha.org

National Museum of American History
Smithsonian Institution
Washington, DC 20560
www.si.edu

Plimoth Plantation
P.O. Box 1620
Plymouth, MA 02362
www.plimoth.org

Rose Center for Earth and Space
American Museum of Natural History
81st St. at Central Park West
New York, NY 10024
www.amnh.org/rose/haydenplanetarium

Smithsonian Institution
P.O. Box 37012
SI Bldg., Rm. 153, MRC 010
Washington, DC 20013-7012
www.si.edu

Appendix D

Park Service Offices

Contact the appropriate office in your area for information about career or volunteer opportunities with the Park Service in the United States and with Parks Canada.

U.S. National Park Service Regional Offices

National Park Service
Alaska Regional Office
2525 Gambell St., Rm. 107
Anchorage, AK 99503-2892
(Manages all the park units in Alaska)

National Park Service
Intermountain Regional Office
12795 Alameda Pkwy.
Denver, CO 80225-0287
(Manages all the park units in Arizona, Colorado, Montana, New Mexico, Oklahoma, Texas, Utah, and Wyoming)

National Park Service
Midwest Regional Office
1709 Jackson St.
Omaha, NE 68102
(Manages all the park units in Arkansas, Illinois, Indiana, Iowa, Kansas, Michigan, Minnesota, Missouri, Nebraska, North Dakota, Ohio, South Dakota, and Wisconsin)

National Park Service
National Capital Regional Office
1100 Ohio Dr. SW
Washington, DC 20242
(Manages all the park units in the District of Columbia, Maryland, Virginia, and West Virginia)

National Park Service
Northeast Regional Office
U.S. Custom House
200 Chestnut St., Rm. 322
Philadelphia, PA 19106
(Manages all the park units in Connecticut, Maine, Massachusetts, New Hampshire, New Jersey, New York, Rhode Island, and Vermont)

National Park Service
Pacific West Regional Office
1111 Jackson Center, Ste. 700
Oakland, CA 94607
(Manages all the park units in California, Hawaii, Idaho, Nevada, Oregon, and Washington)

National Park Service
Southeast Regional Office
75 Spring St. SW, Ste. 1130
Atlanta, GA 30303
(Manages all the park units in Alabama, Florida, Georgia, Kentucky, Louisiana, Mississippi, North Carolina, Puerto Rico, South Carolina, Tennessee, and the Virgin Islands)

Parks Canada Offices

National Office
25 Eddy St.
Hull, QC K1A 0M5

Calgary Service Center
220 4th Ave. SE, Rm. 552
Calgary, AB T2P 3H8
(Manages all sites in Alberta)

Cornwall Service Center
111 Water St. East
Cornwall, ON K6H 6S3
(Manages all sites in Ontario)

Halifax Service Center
1864 Upper Water St.
Halifax, NS B3J 1S9
(Manages sites in Labrador, New Brunswick, Newfoundland, Nova Scotia, and Prince Edward Island)

Quebec City Service Center
3 Passage du Chien d'Or
P.O. Box 6060, Haute-Ville
Quebec City, QC G1R 4V7
(Manages all sites in Quebec)

Vancouver Service Center
300-300 W. Georgia St.
Vancouver, BC V6B 6C6
(Manages all sites in British Columbia and the Yukon)

Winnipeg Service Center
45 Forks Market Rd.
Winnipeg, MB R3C 4T6
(Manages all sites in Manitoba, Northwest Territories, and
Saskatchewan)

Selected Reading

The following titles provide further information on careers covered in this book. These are only a small sample of the resources available for those interested in pursuing any of the many career possibilities available in museums.

American Museum of Natural History. *Rose Center for Earth and Space: A Museum for the 21st Century*. New York: American Museum of Natural History, 2001.

Bernardin, Tom. *The Ellis Island Immigrant Cookbook*. New York: Tom Bernardin Inc., 2004.

Bradford, William. *Bradford's History of Plimoth Plantation from the Original Manuscript*. Kila, Mont.: Kessinger Publishing, 2004.

Brinkley, M. Kent and Gordon W. Chappell. *The Gardens of Colonial Williamsburg*. Williamsburg, Va.: Colonial Williamsburg Foundation, 2005.

Camenson, Blythe. *Careers for History Buffs*, 2nd ed. Chicago: McGraw-Hill, 2002.

Fagan, Bryan M. *Archaeology: A Brief Introduction*, 8th ed. Upper Saddle River, N.J.: Prentice Hall, 2002.

Graduate Guides (Peterson's Graduate and Professional Programs). Lawrenceville, N.J.: Peterson's Guides, 2005.

Hall, Maggie. *St. Augustine (Images of America: Florida)*. Mount Pleasant, S.C.: Arcadia Publishing, 2002.

Howard, Hugh. *The Historic Homes of Williamsburg*. New York: Harry N. Abrams, Inc., 2004.

Hunter, Gregory S. *Developing and Maintaining Practical Archives*, 2nd ed. New York: Neal Schuman Publishers, 2003.

Lubar, Steven D. *Legacies: Collecting America's History at the Smithsonian*. Washington, DC: Smithsonian Books, 2001.

Official Museum Directory, 2006. New Brunswick, N.J.: National Register Publishing, 2005.

Renick, Barbara. *Genealogy 101: How to Trace Your Family's History and Heritage*. Nashville: Rutledge Hill Press, 2003.

Thackray, John and Bob Press. *The Natural History Museum: Nature's Treasure House*. London: The Natural History Museum, 2001.

About the Author

A FULL-TIME WRITER of career books, Blythe Camenson wants to help job seekers make educated choices. She believes that with enough information, readers can find long-term, satisfying careers, so she researches traditional as well as unusual occupations, talking to a variety of professionals about what their jobs are like. In her books she includes firsthand accounts from people who can reveal what to expect in each occupation—the upsides as well as the down.

Camenson's interests range from history and photography to writing novels. She is also the director of Fiction Writer's Connection, an organization providing support to new and published writers.

Camenson was educated in Boston, earning her B.A. in English and psychology from the University of Massachusetts and her M.Ed. in counseling from Northeastern University.

In addition to *Opportunities in Museum Careers*, the books she has written for McGraw-Hill include *Careers for History Buffs, Careers for Plant Lovers, Careers for Health Nuts, Opportunities in Teaching English to Speakers of Other Languages,* and *Great Jobs for Communications Majors.*